Learner-Centered Classroom Practices and Assessments

We dedicate this book to all the great teachers we have met around the world, and to all who have embraced the Learner-Centered Principles and Model. Thanks for making a difference!

Learner-Centered Classroom Practices and Assessments

Maximizing Student Motivation, Learning, and Achievement

BARBARA L. McCOMBS

LYNDA MILLER

CORWIN PRESS
A SAGE Publications Company
Thousand Oaks, CA 91320

For information:

Corwin Press
A Sage Publications Company
2455 Teller Road
Thousand Oaks, California 91320
www.corwinpress.com

Sage Publications Ltd.
1 Oliver's Yard
55 City Road
London EC1Y 1SP
United Kingdom

Sage Publications India Pvt. Ltd.
B-42, Panchsheel Enclave
Post Box 4109
New Delhi 110 017 India

Printed in the United States of America

Library of Congress Cataloging-in-Publication Data

McCombs, Barbara L.
Learner-centered classroom practices and assessments: Maximizing student motivation, learning, and achievement/Barbara L. McCombs and Lynda Miller.
    p. cm.
Includes bibliographical references and index.
ISBN: 1-4129-2690-4 or 978-1-4129-2690-4
ISBN: 1-4129-2691-2 or 978-1-4129-2691-1
    1. Learning, Psychology of. 2. Individualized instruction. 3. Teaching.
I. Miller, Lynda. II. Title.
LB1060.M38 2007
370.15'23—dc22   2006017032

This book is printed on acid-free paper.

06 07 08 09 10 10 9 8 7 6 5 4 3 2 1

Acquisitions Editor:	Faye Zucker
Editorial Assistants:	Gem Rabanera
	Charline Wu
Production Editor:	Beth A. Bernstein
Copy Editor:	Diana Breti
Typesetter:	C&M Digitals (P) Ltd.
Proofreader:	Andrea Martin
Indexer:	Rick Hurd
Cover Designer:	Rose Storey
Graphic Designer:	Lisa Riley

Contents

Preface   ix

Acknowledgments   xii

About the Authors   xv

1. What We Know About Learning   1
   How Do You Learn Best?   2
   What Does the Evidence Show About
      Supporting Natural Learning?   4
   Teachers and Students as Co-Learners: An Invitation   7
   What's Next?   9

**2. What Is Learner Centered From an
Evidence-Based Perspective?**   15
   What Does "Learner Centered" Mean?   15
   Seeing the Big Picture: Education as a Complex Living System   17
   Domains of Schools as Living Systems   19
   The Learner-Centered Model   21
   What Are the Learner-Centered Principles?   24
   Factors Affecting Learners and Learning   32
   What's Next?   32

**3. What Teachers and Students
Tell Us About Learner-Centered Practices**   33
   What Teachers Have Recognized About the LCPs   33
   Translating the LCPs Into Practice   33
   The LCPs, Testing, and Accountability   34
   What Do the LCPs Mean for Teaching and Learning?   35
   What the Evidence Shows:
     Characteristics of Effective Teachers   36
   What Students Say   36
   Strategies for Honoring Student Voice   38
     Forming a Student Forum   39
     Involving Students in Action Research Projects   40
   Students as Meaningful Partners: International Evidence   41
   Reflection   42
   What's Next?   42

4. The Learner-Centered Principles: One by One   45
   Domain 1: Cognitive and Metacognitive Factors   46

LCP 1: Nature of the Learning Process 47
LCP 2: Goals of the Learning Process 47
LCP 3: Construction of Knowledge 49
LCP 4: Strategic Thinking 49
LCP 5: Thinking About Thinking 50
LCP 6: Context of Learning 51
Domain 2: Motivational and Affective Factors 52
LCP 7: Motivational and Emotional
          Influences on Learning 52
LCP 8: Intrinsic Motivation to Learn 53
LCP 9: Effects of Motivation on Effort 54
Domain 3: Developmental and Social Factors 55
LCP 10: Developmental Influence on Learning 56
LCP 11: Social Influences on Learning 57
Domain 4: Individual Differences Factors 58
LCP 12: Individual Differences in Learning 59
LCP 13: Learning and Diversity 60
LCP 14: Standards and Assessment 62
Finding Examples of LCPs in Your Own Practices 63
What's Next? 67

5. Learner-Centered Practices **71**
Turning Principles Into Practices 72
Glasser's Six Conditions for Quality Schoolwork 74
Classroom Climate 75
Relevance of Learner-Centered Practices
    in the Context of Standards and Assessment 78
The Achievement Gap Issue 79
What Students Say About the Achievement Gap 81
Reflection 85
What's Next? 86

6. Effective Learner-Centered Practices **87**
Effective Learner-Centered Practices for Students in K–3 87
Effective Learner-Centered Practices for Students in Grades 4–12 89
What Happened to "Classroom Management"? 93
Strategies for Creating Learner-Centered, Resilient Classrooms 96
Insights and Reflections: What Needs to Change in My
    Classroom? 101
What's Next? 101

7. What Tools Do I Need to Become Learner Centered? **103**
Who's in Charge of My Learning? 105
Who's in Charge of Students' Learning? 107
Implications for Practice 112
Implications for Policy 113
The Learner-Centered Surveys 115

    Characteristics of Learner-Centered Tools 115
    The Assessment of Learner-Centered Practices (ALCP):
       Tools for Creating Learner-Centered Classrooms
       and Departments 117
    Research-Validated Definition of "Learner Centered" 120
ALCP Feedback Process for Teachers 121
Understanding Sample ALCP Feedback: Table of Teacher Variables
    Compared to the Learner-Centered Rubric for One Teacher 123
Becoming a Magnet for Change in My School and District 126
Reassessing My Beliefs 129
What Is My Vision for Schools? 129
My Plan for a Learner-Centered Classroom 135
How Can I Manage Resistance to Change? 136
Obtaining the Necessary Support for Learner-Centered Schools 138
Where Do I Go From Here? 142

Resource A: Teacher Strategy Ideas **147**

Resource B: Contacts: Learner-Centered Projects and Schools **153**

Resource C: Books and Journals Worth a Read **155**

Resource D: Learner-Centered Glossary: Some Definitions **157**

References **161**

Index **173**

Preface

Our purpose in this book is to remind you of what you already know and then tell you about the research evidence that supports your knowledge. We hope this "reminder" will empower you to utilize the experiential, intuitive knowledge you already have in ways that can make a positive difference for your students and yourself. We know from hundreds of teachers we have worked with that giving yourself permission to do what you know is best will help you regain the sense of hope and optimism you had when you first entered the teaching profession (minus the fear that you probably felt the first day you entered your own classroom).

You already know that, when people—students, teachers, administrators, parents—are actively engaged in learning that taps into their creativity and curiosity, they are engaged in changing. Viewed in this way, change is synonymous with learning and learning with change. Learning and change need not be mandated or resisted; rather, they are irresistible because they are natural consequences of being alive. Your job as a teacher and a learner is to figure out how best to support the natural processes of learning and change in teaching and learning. You will rediscover that both learning and change are part of a continuous journey—the journey to lifelong learning, continuous change, and improvement.

The ideas and tools we describe in this book are also meant to support you in maintaining or regaining your equilibrium as a teacher of students. The tools we offer will validate you as a learner-teacher, confirm what you already know, and provide you with the means to withstand the effects of poorly designed educational policies, environments, or paradigms.

Moving From Fear to Optimism

The best teachers throughout human history have understood the value of learning. They have also understood that people differ in how they learn, what they learn, and what motivates them to learn. These teachers have also known that the most effective way to teach is to focus on individual learners—their needs, interests, and particular talents or learning capacities. These special teachers have known how to challenge learners to achieve at their highest levels and how to provide the caring, mentoring, and modeling needed for learners to continue to push their limits and learning potentials.

Some of these early special teachers (e.g., Socrates, Plato, Confucius) and their teaching methods (e.g., questioning, analogies, parables) have been recorded in historical accounts. However, only recently has the scientific basis for particular teaching philosophies and methods been documented. This base of scientific evidence is particularly necessary in the twenty-first entury, as educational policy has so far been dominated by demands for accountability, increased student achievement, teacher quality, and evidence-based best practices stemming from rigorous scientific research.

On the down side, however, the current policies surrounding educational reform have, for many students, families, and teachers, produced a climate of fear. Large numbers of teachers and students are experiencing feelings of failure, demoralization, alienation, and fear. Many quality teachers are leaving their chosen profession, and high numbers of able students are dropping out of school because of the negative environments created in many schools and classrooms by an educational agenda focused primarily on testing and accountability.

This book is intended to counteract and help balance the current negative agenda and to provide you with a sense of hope and reconnection with the ways you can make a difference with the students you teach. It will also help you achieve a necessary balance between (a) high standards and a focus on content and (b) research-validated principles and practices that focus on learners and learning.

In this book, we present evidence of positive, practical, research-based options for meeting current national and state demands for high learning standards and increased teacher and school accountability. We will show you how it is possible for students to reach high levels of achievement without being subjected to fear-based, punitive methods. We describe how you and your students can meet the rigorous academic curricula and testing requirements in core subject areas without losing the joy of learning and teaching. We also focus on how the Learner-Centered Psychological Principles (LCPs) can be used to redesign educational practices in your classroom, school, and district. We use a variety of examples to highlight how to implement the LCPs, and we share success stories to illustrate the use of the LCPs in classrooms and schools in the United States and other countries around the world.

Evidence-Based Practices

We have written this book to help teachers at all levels of the educational system—from preschool through postsecondary—understand the evidence base for effective teaching strategies that can reach all learners. The evidence is clear: These learner-centered strategies inspire students' natural motivation for lifelong learning and for reaching their highest achievement levels.

Throughout this book we'll show you the evidence demonstrating positive outcomes—both academic and nonacademic—that have been achieved through using learner-centered practices. The illustrations we use throughout this book showing the efficacy of learner-centered practices are based on research that applies not only to increased learning and academic achievement, but also to the development of social and emotional learning skills, including skills for lifelong learning. Validated by thorough and systematic research over an extended period of time, a set of psychological principles, the LCPs, has emerged. These principles, which underlie learner-centered teaching, are best understood as operating on two levels.

1. They define the nature of learning, as well as the various cognitive, metacognitive, affective, motivational, and social processes that support learning.

2. They incorporate the developmental and other individual differences that define unique learner needs and learning experiences.

Because of the strong research evidence supporting the Learner-Centered Psychological Principles (LCPs), the American Psychological Association (APA) in 1997 adopted them as a framework for redesigning K–20 education. These principles, representing over a century of research, have been advocated by many well-known educators who have emphasized various aspects of the principles. Many of you will recognize the LCPs in the educational reform ideas of educators such as John Dewey, Jerome Bruner, and Joseph Schwab, among others. These educators recognized, like many of the ancient teachers, that learning and motivation are natural processes and that learners must be the focus of the learning process in order for them to be fully engaged in the learning process. Similarly, learners must see that what is being learned is meaningful and relevant to their personal and life interests, which results in a natural motivation to learn. It is our hope that you will find the content of our book meaningful, relevant, and motivating as well, and we welcome you on your journey!

Acknowledgments

The opportunity to share our work with teachers and other educators fills us with gratitude for the many friends, relatives, and professional mentors who have blessed us throughout our lives. It is truly to them that the ideas here had their genesis. You will see their work cited throughout this book.

From Barbara

My deepest gratitude goes to my parents. Their unconditional love and support helped me not only believe in myself and my gifts, but also helped enhance my curiosity, creativity, and lifelong love of learning. They also helped me realize that these qualities can be nourished and further developed in all learners. And to this, I have dedicated my professional life.

Very special thanks are due my twin sister for her emotional support and her excellent editorial skills. She took what Lynda and I created and made it even better. And, of course, without my co-author Lynda's special talents, teaching background, and wonderful writing skills, this book would not have been possible.

My husband and children have also been a source of support and inspiration for this book. They deserve my very personal thanks and it is for them and my grandchildren that I have my greatest hopes that the message of this book will be realized.

I reserve my last thanks for our editor, Faye Zucker. Her belief in this message and this book made my dream come true.

From Lynda

My greatest appreciation and gratitude go to those students who, many years ago (I refuse to say how many!), turned most of my assumptions about learners and learning upside down so that I could actually think about both in a fresh, productive way. This profound shake-up occurred with my first teaching assignment—a classroom of seventh graders to whom I was to teach English. Never mind that for a good number of them, their primary language was Spanish, while my first language was English and my almost-second one French. And never mind that the district had no curriculum for seventh-grade English, meaning I was free to create my own, based on what I had learned in my major during college, English Language and Literature. I was not quite so naïve as to expect my students to automatically have an interest in the vagaries (and niceties) of the English language or in the long history of fine English writers, but my training had prepared me to believe that to proceed in this world, my students would have to become adept at manipulating the language and understanding the literature.

You can probably guess what happened. The short version is that I quickly learned that the pedagogy I had been taught just didn't work with these kids because it was far removed from what was relevant and meaningful in their lives. What did work? Finding out what their experiences and interests were and using those as the basis from which to explore themes and develop skills. In other words, what worked was making learning and learners, including myself, the focus of everything that transpired in our classroom. I have those students to thank for teaching me to flip the traditional instructional model on its head and look at things upside down, which becomes right side up in no time at all.

I want to express my gratitude and admiration to Barbara, whose thoughtful and careful work on learner-centered practices made this book possible. Working together has been one of the easiest, most pleasurable collaborations I've ever encountered. Thank you, Barbara, for making this such a delicious experience. I look forward to many more collaborations and opportunities to bring together "old" learnings with the ever-emerging new and exciting ones.

To Jim Patton, friend and colleague, a special thank you for your encouragement and for your deep network that led Barbara and me to Corwin Press.

We owe special thanks to Faye Zucker, our editor *par extraordinaire,* whose belief in this book renews our hope that changing some of the most egregious practices currently employed in our schools is, indeed, possible. Faye's thoughtful and humorous feedback throughout the writing process has helped make this a much better book than it would have been without her. Thank you, Faye.

And, finally, thanks also go to Gem Rabanera and Charline Wu, editorial assistants at Corwin Press; Beth Bernstein, production editor; and Diana Breti, copyeditor, for their ability to understand what we meant even when it wasn't clear and to bring the manuscript into perfect order.

Corwin Press would like to thank the following reviewers for their contributions to this book:

Lesley Bartlett, Assistant Professor, Teachers College, Columbia University, New York, NY

Betty Brandenburg Yundt, Teacher, Walker Intermediate School, Fort Knox, KY

Leonard Burrello, Director, Forum on Education at Indiana University

Judi Elman, English Teacher, Highland Park High School, Highland Park, IL

Ellen Herbert, Teacher, Longview High School, Longview, TX

Peter Hoffman-Kipp, Faculty Advisor, Center X in the UCLA Graduate School of Education and Information Studies, University of California, Los Angeles

Manisha Javeri, Assistant Professor, Applied and Advanced Studies in Education, California State University, Los Angeles

Carmen Shields, Professor, Nipissing University, North Bay, ON, Canada

Brigitte Tennis, Head Mistress & Seventh Grade Teacher, Stella Schola Middle School, Redmond, WA

About the Authors

Barbara L. McCombs, PhD, is a Senior Research Scientist at the University of Denver Research Institute located on the University of Denver's campus in Denver, Colorado. She also directs the Human Motivation, Learning, and Development Center at the Denver Research Institute, which focuses on Professional Development of Educators, School Violence Prevention, Systemic Educational Reform, and Personal and Organizational Change. Her current research is directed at new models of teaching and learning, including transformational teacher development approaches and the use of technology as a primary tool for empowering youth.

Dr. McCombs is the author of numerous book chapters and journal articles. She is also the primary author of the *Learner-Centered Psychological Principles: Guidelines for School Redesign and Reform* being disseminated by the American Psychological Association's Task Force on Psychology in Education. Her concept of a K–20 seamless professional development model is described in her book, co-authored with Jo Sue Whisler, *The Learner-Centered Classroom and School: Strategies for Enhancing Student Motivation and Achievement.* Dr. McCombs is also the primary editor for the American Psychological Association's *Psychology in the Classroom: A Series for Teachers and Teacher Educators.*

Lynda Miller, PhD, is an independent scholar whose work focuses on synthesizing research in cognition, learning, intelligence, and language development for application in schools and classrooms. Dr. Miller's work emphasizes the importance of matching students' unique patterns of strengths and motivations with appropriately selected instructional materials and methods. Throughout her professional career, Dr. Miller has provided comprehensive consultation to a variety of educational organizations, entities, and agencies in the United States, Canada, and Europe.

Dr. Miller's publications include *What We Call Smart: A New Narrative for Intelligence and Learning,* an extended essay on how to shift from a rhetoric based on measuring and comparing people's intelligence and learning abilities to a rhetoric based on identifying and describing the individual strengths and talents that underlie each person's cognition and learning. She is the co-author, with Lauren Hoffman, PhD, of *Linking IEPs to State Learning Standards: A Step-By-Step Guide;* and with Chris Newbill, PhD, of *Section 504 in the Classroom: Designing and Implementing Accommodation Plans.* Dr. Miller co-authored with James Gilliam, PhD the *Pragmatic Language Skills Inventory,* a classroom-based instrument that measures students' personal, classroom, and social language skills.

Along with her professional work, Dr. Miller is a painter and Web designer. She enjoys hiking, rollerblading, playing with her dog and cat, and enjoying convivial conversations with family and friends.

1

What We Know About Learning

Imagine a situation in which something very dear to you (e.g., your job, your family, your health) depends on your ability to correctly identify what is pictured in Figure 1.1.

Needless to say, in this hypothetical situation, you're highly motivated to figure out what is being shown in the picture. However, the picture is only obvious to approximately 10% of people; the other 90% can figure it out with some instruction. What sort of instruction would be most likely to result in your figuring out the picture?

Here's what a group of teachers said when they were asked this question after seeing this picture:

"I learn best by having it explained to me."

"Tell me how the picture is constructed so I can figure it out on my own."

"Tell me what it's supposed to be."

"Show me another one like it."

"Talking to other people about it helps me learn."

"Give me some paper so I can draw around the black areas."

"I need to read more information about how the picture works."

"Give me some options to choose from."

"I want to be under my headphones, listening to music, and not listening to anybody else."

"Let me make some guesses, and you tell me if I'm close."

What would you say? Something similar to what these other teachers said, or something entirely different? The point is that although we share some processes in common, each person approaches a learning task in a unique way. The key component, however, is that in figuring out the picture, each of us is engaged in **learning**.

Take a moment to look at Figure 1.1 again. Now, select from the approaches below to figure out what the picture is.

- Take different visual perspectives (i.e., hold it different distances

Figure 1.1

from your eyes or look at it out of the corner of your eye) to see whether you can figure it out.

- Read what other people think it is (turn to Note 1 in the Chapter 1 Notes).
- See another picture like it (turn to Note 2 in the Chapter 1 Notes).
- Read information about how the picture was constructed (turn to Note 3 in the Chapter 1 Notes).
- Try drawing "wholes" around pieces of the picture (turn to Note 4 in the Chapter 1 Notes for another copy of the picture you can draw on).
- Listen to some music while you look at the picture (you're on your own here).
- Read a set of words describing the picture (turn to Note 5 in the Chapter 1 Notes and follow the instructions for covering the list so you can read the words one by one).

Once you've figured out the picture, reflect for a moment on the learning strategies you used. We'll return to this puzzle picture later, and don't worry if you don't see the picture; some people never see it (there's a picture in Note 6 to show you what the "answer" is). And, if you're curious about the second picture, Note 7 shows the "answer."

How Do You Learn Best?

How do you learn best? Take a minute or two to think about how you approached the puzzle picture. What was the first strategy you used to figure it out? Did that strategy work? If not, what did you try next? Did that work? If not, how did you feel? Did you want to give up? Were you angry? Did you skip ahead? Did you turn to Note 6 to see what the "answer" was? Were you reassured by our telling you not to worry if you didn't see the picture? Did you reserve judgment, thinking we might be playing a trick on you? Or are you one of the 10% of people who see the "answer" right away? The answers to these questions offer some insight into how you like to approach learning something new and what you do when the process is not necessarily immediate or easy (unless you're in that 10% group).

Another way to gain insight into how you learn best is to consider your responses to these questions:

- What do you typically do to reduce stress? Do you like to be alone? Listen to or create music? Read? Walk/sit in a natural setting? Organize your closets/drawers/workshop/files/calendar? Talk to friends? Look at art? Draw, paint, sculpt, make a piece of furniture? Dance? Watch a sports event? Volunteer in a community organization or agency? Get a massage? Play video games? Surf the Internet?

- How do you play? Do you like to play by yourself? With animals? With other people? What form does your play take? Is it organized and scripted (e.g., an athletic activity of some sort)? Or is it more spontaneous (e.g., skipping stones on water, tossing a Frisbee with a friend, going to a movie)? Is your play physical? Musical? Does it involve language (e.g., Do you like to play with words)? Do you like to play with colors, forms, textures? Do you like to play with different ways to organize things (e.g., time, events, objects, ideas)? Do you like to play with numbers or numerical concepts? Do you

enjoy using new technologies and Web-based tools?

- What sorts of things in your life do you like to think about and plan? For instance, do you enjoy planning social gatherings? If so, which aspects are most enjoyable? Thinking about who will be there and the dynamics among people? Planning the decorations and food? Thinking about the clothing everyone will wear? Which sorts of things do you dread doing? Balancing your checkbook? Talking to a family member about something difficult? Exercising? Being alone? Being in social situations? Playing party games?

- Do you prefer working on projects with other people, or do you prefer working by yourself? If you work with others, is it easy for you to explain your ideas and thoughts? Which role(s) do you typically take: leader, organizer, idea generator, explainer, recorder, detail person, emotional support person? If you prefer working alone, how do you approach a new project? What do you usually do first? Which part of working alone do you most enjoy?

- Do you always approach problems or new learning in the same way, or do you like to try new approaches to see how they work? Over your lifetime, have you changed the way you like to learn and experience new things? Are your learning strengths different from what they were when you were a teenager? A young(er) adult?

- Do you like to know why you should bother to learn new skills, knowledge, or processes? That is, before you commit to learning something new, do you analyze its relevance, value, cost, and short-term and long-term contributions to your life?

When thinking about your responses to these questions, consider how you feel when you find yourself in learning situations in which your learning preferences are recognized, valued, supported, and extended. Alternately, think about how you feel when your learning preferences are overlooked, dismissed, or worse, denigrated. If you're like most people, you feel energized and creative when you're in learning environments that support how you learn best, and you feel angry, depressed, or even hopeless when you find yourself in learning contexts that do not support how you learn best.

Most of us go into teaching because we believe we can make a positive difference in young people's lives. For many of us, we share a belief in students' curiosity and desire to learn, we want to support them as lifelong learners, and we desire to help students develop into competent and responsible adults. We undertake the job of educating students out of a commitment to the greater good of our society, knowing that supporting students in their development as learners leads to citizens who care about not just themselves and their own communities, but other people and societies as well.

Today, in many parts of the United States, schools are no longer organized to support students' inherent curiosity, desire to learn, and motivation to develop responsibility for their learning. Reflecting on how you tried to solve the puzzle picture and your responses to the questions that followed, imagine how students feel when they have few—or no—opportunities to explore learning, discover how they learn best, try out different approaches to solving problems, work independently and with teammates on projects that interest them, determine the relevance of what they are learning to their lives, and analyze the benefits of their learning to their short- and long-term goals for themselves. Imagine how you would feel if you were in their shoes. Would you feel motivated to learn what someone else thinks is best for you? Would you feel motivated to learn from someone who tells you what you need to know, in spite of the fact that he or she knows little or nothing about you and your life, dreams, hopes, and goals?

What Does the Evidence Show About Supporting Natural Learning?

From our research as well as that of others who have explored differences in what learning looks like in and out of school settings, several things have become obvious (e.g., McCombs, 2001, 2004b; Zimmerman & Schunk, 2001). Real-life learning from the learner's perspective is often playful, recursive and nonlinear, engaging, self-directed, and meaningful. But why are the natural processes of motivation and learning seen in real life rarely seen in most school settings? The research shows that self-motivated learning is only possible in contexts that provide the learner with **choice** and **control**. When students have choice and are allowed to control major aspects of their learning (such as what topics to pursue, how and when to study, and outcomes to achieve) they are more likely to self-regulate their thinking and learning processes than when they have little or no choice or control.

Recall how you approached "solving" the picture puzzle at the beginning of this chapter. Imagine how you would have approached solving it if we had said you needed to learn how to solve puzzles of this type because you'd need to know how to do it later in your life. Imagine, too, how you would have approached the problem if we had told you that you had no choice about learning how to do it.

The research indicates that schools need to offer person-centered models of learning that incorporate challenging learning experiences. School learning experiences should prepare learners to be knowledge producers, knowledge users, and socially responsible citizens. Given the research evidence, a natural question to ask is whether the socially valued academic knowledge and skills standards currently in vogue are sufficient for educating students for the twenty-first-century world, where content is so abundant that it makes a poor foundation for an educational system. The scarce commodities are context, meaning, and successful communication with others. The purposes of education that prepares learners for the world outside school are to teach learners how to communicate with others, find relevant and accurate information for the task at hand, and become co-learners with teachers and peers in diverse settings beyond school walls.

Moving toward this vision requires fresh concepts, validated by evidence from careful research, that define the learning process and the evolving purposes of education. It also requires rethinking current directions and practices. While maintaining high standards in the learning of desired content and skills, the learner, learning process, and learning environment must not be neglected if we are to adequately prepare students for productive and healthy futures. Consequently, state and national standards must be critically reevaluated in terms of what is necessary to prepare students to be knowledgeable, responsible, and caring citizens. Standards must move beyond knowledge conservation to incorporate knowledge creation and production (Hannafin, 1999). The current focus on content must be balanced with a focus on individual learners and their holistic learning needs in an increasingly complex and fast-changing world.

Educators have long argued that content alone does not prepare students to be successful workers in the global economy or effective citizens in the global village (McLuhan, 1989; Tomlinson, 1999). What is needed are learner-centered models of schooling that promote autonomy, personal responsibility, and trust, as well as the broader base of knowledge that allows students to be more than low-level knowledge reproducers. Current models of school that focus on firm control of students and rote memorization promote compliance with directives, inability and unwillingness to question authority, and dependence and fragility as a lifelong learner. In contrast, learner-centered models contribute to the development of students who are the knowledge producers and critical thinkers who participate actively and productively both in their local societies and the global community. To become knowledge producers and critical thinkers, students must experience schooling practices in which they are active partners with caring adults in governance and learning activities. Through their experiences in school, they must experience and help create social justice; they must have opportunities to learn ethical decision making through partnering with the adults in their schools and communities.

The needs of learners—including teachers as learners—are changing and require our attention in order to address problems such as school dropout and teacher departures from the profession, both consequences of learner alienation. Ryan and Deci (2000) maintain that alienation in any age population is caused by failing to provide supports for competence, autonomy, and relatedness. Preparing teachers to meet these needs for themselves and their students is essential to healthy development and to creating contexts that engender individual commitment, effort, and high-quality performance. Unfortunately, there are numerous examples in the current educational reform agenda of coercive and punitive consequences for students, teachers, and administrators when students fail to achieve educational standards on state and national tests. The time has come for a research-based model that addresses these learner needs while also addressing high standards of performance for all learners.

A recent national study of low socioeconomic status (SES) and minority elementary students indicated that the most powerful school characteristics for promoting resiliency (academic success) included a supportive school environment model that was safe and orderly and that promoted positive student-teacher relationships (Borman & Overman, 2004). Students in these environments displayed greater engagement in academic activities, a stronger sense of math efficacy, higher self-esteem, and a more positive outlook toward school. These models are particularly needed in today's culture, which has fewer and less stable family and social institutions that promote resilience. Schools can help meet these needs to the extent that they are focused on learner needs that go beyond academic competence (Phillips, 1997).

A review of alternative educational models examined learner-centered, progressive, and holistic education (Martin, 2002). Growing numbers of alternative schools fit within this broad category and include democratic and free schools, folk education, Quaker schools, home schooling/unschooling/deschooling, Krishnamurti schools, Montessori education, open schools, and Waldorf schools. This diversity of alternatives to mainstream or traditional education is in keeping with social values that include pluralism and diversity, a more sustainable world, and just democracy. The alternative models tend *not* to be rooted in an overly rational or objective way of knowing; in addition, they acknowledge interdependencies and values, and they incorporate the emotional, ecological, spiritual, physical, social, and intellectual aspects of living that are reflected in schooling (Forbes, 1999). These learner-based models address the needs of the whole child in balance with the needs of the community and society. They hold in common a respect for diversity and different philosophical beliefs about what it means to live, learn, love, and grow in today's society. They are all "person-centered" approaches expressed in a diversity of ways. What makes "learner-centered" education transformative (holistic) is its recognition that meaning is co-constructed and that self-regulation occurs through interdependence, with a focus on being and becoming fully functioning.

Teachers and Students as Co-Learners: An Invitation

Learner-centered teachers not only know the subject matter they are teaching; they also understand that they—along with their students—are learners. The most effective teachers know how to flexibly shift their role from teacher to expert learner to beginning learner. As co-learners, they can share the ownership of learning with their students as appropriate. They model effective learning processes as they help students understand how to assume increased responsibility for their learning. And, learner-centered teachers know which knowledge and skills they want students to acquire and the best methods for facilitating the learning process for individual learners with diverse learning interests and needs.

Teaching practices that are "learner-centered" stem from the understanding that each student needs to feel known, respected, cared about, and supported. Students whose teachers use learner-centered practices are aware that their unique learning needs, interests, and talents are being considered and are valued and respected. They are partners with teachers in the learning process. As a result, they feel honored, supported, and have a sense of ownership of their learning. In the process, students' natural motivation to learn emerges.

When an educational paradigm or reform agenda puts something other than the learner at the center of instructional decision making, all learners—teachers included—suffer. They know that the system is not about them and is not responsive to their needs. From learners' perspectives, the system is out of balance if knowledge (content standards) or learning (performance skills and achievement measures) is at the center of instructional decision making. In such a system, learners recognize they are not important because who they are and what they need are not at the heart of the learning process. At worst, they feel left out, ignored, or alienated; at best, they feel the system is impersonal and irrelevant. In either case, learning and motivation to learn suffer. Students and teachers alike begin to disengage from the learning process.

> If kids feel connected, if they feel part of a community where they're respected and valued, they'll be more likely to stay in school . . . and succeed. (Social studies teacher we have worked with in a learner-centered high school)

In learner-centered systems, teachers model lifelong and continuous learning for their students. They also assume leadership roles and serve as key constituents in the educational system (students, teachers, other school staff, parents, community members) to support students in a lifelong learning process of continuous growth and improvement. Teachers in learner-centered systems fundamentally understand the relational nature of learning. That is, they understand that at its core, learning is relational in two ways: (1) individual learners attempt to make personal meaning from information and experiences and (2) strong student-teacher relationships provide a positive climate out of which natural learning and motivation emerge.

School cultures based on learners, that is, school cultures focused on personalized learning, use collaboration between teachers and students working together to develop meaningful learning activities (Keefe & Jenkins, 2002). In these schools, there is a collective responsibility for student learning and a focus on high morale as well as high academic achievement. Learning environments in these schools are "thoughtful" in the sense that they support conversation, learning by doing, apprenticeship experiences, and authentic student achievement. Instruction is organized to focus on a few important topics in integrated and coherent ways that provide continuity and time for inquiry, interactive dialogue, and quality of thought rather than the need for "right" answers. Teachers and students have input into the way time is used, with an emphasis on performance rather than time so that students have more opportunities to make choices in curriculum and instruction.

Schools organized around personalized instruction focus on renewal, or how learner growth in knowledge and self-awareness can lead to wisdom and collective responsibility, how to create creative and supportive educational environments, and how to engage learners in critical inquiry and reflection about educational practice (Keefe & Jenkins, 2002). In these personalized learning environments, the school is organized to take individual learner characteristics and needs into account and to use flexible instructional practices that address individual learning strengths. The basic premise is that personalized instruction must begin with a knowledge of the learner across a variety of areas, including developmental characteristics, learning styles, and learning histories as well as personal interests and other background characteristics.

Palmer (1999) argues that we need to acknowledge that teaching and learning involve not only intellect and emotion, but also the human spirit. He believes that teaching and learning aren't either intellectual *or* spiritual. He contends that teachers—regardless of their subject matter and who their students are—end up teaching who they are. The biggest challenge is to provide teachers with adequate time and support to reflect on questions worth living and sharing with their students.

You already know that time for self-reflection can renew and transform your teaching practices and the ways you relate to yourself and others. We teachers need opportunities to learn and change our minds. All of us can benefit from assessing our fundamental beliefs and assumptions about learners, learning, and teaching. If you are at the beginning of your teaching career, you will be able to incorporate what you learn from this book into your daily practice in a way that enriches you and your students. If you're an experienced teacher, you will be able to identify those learner-centered practices you already use in your classroom and ways to begin using those you haven't used before.

One of the most powerful aspects of using the learner-centered practices we describe in this book is the opportunity to experience first hand the importance of your students' perspectives on whether your teaching practices are meeting their academic and nonacademic learning needs. We encourage you to reflect on what you learn from your self-assessment and your students' perspectives on your teaching in order to determine how you can best develop positive relationships and learning climates that support your students' learning and motivation.

Sharing power and control with your students and viewing yourself as a learner assists your students in understanding that when learners of any age feel ownership of their learning, by virtue of having a voice and choice, they are more willing to learn and be involved in their learning (McCombs, 2000a). When your learning experiences show this to be the case, you will see the value of providing these experiences for your students. Once you have experienced the results of using the learner-centered principles, you will understand that the most effective learning involves providing your students (and yourself) with opportunities for choice when making personal connections with prior and new knowledge. In this way, you honor both yourself and your students.

As a way to chart your thinking as you read this book, you may wish to start a personal journal to record your ongoing reflections. Throughout the book, we will ask you to reflect as a way to chart your progress as a learner as well as how your learning translates into ideas for your classroom. To help you begin your journaling, you may wish to read Jane Tompkins's essay, "Pedagogy of the Distressed," in which she describes her shift from viewing teaching as the process of dispensing information and learning as the process of receiving it to a perspective of learning as a shared process between teacher and students (Tompkins, 1990). Although Tompkins's experience was in a university setting, the process she describes is that of a teacher becoming learner centered.

Let's go back to the puzzle picture in Figure 1.1. If you had to teach your students how to "solve" pictures like this, how would you construct a lesson (or lessons) that incorporates what you've learned so far about learner-centered practices? How would your lesson (or lessons) reflect the learning strategies that you used to figure out the picture?

What's Next?

In Chapter 2, we describe in detail what we mean by "learner centered," using the perspective of education as a living system, the basic characteristics of schools as complex living systems, the characteristics of the Learner-Centered Model (LCM) and corresponding Learner-Centered Principles (LCPs), what the CPs mean for teaching and learning, what the evidence shows about characteristics of effective teachers, and the major factors affecting learners and learning.

Note 1

Here's what other people have said they think the picture shows:

A panda

A lion

A Dalmatian

Trees and islands

A view from space

A cowboy on a horse

Two people walking

An abstract painting

A girl in a bonnet

Note 2

Here's another picture constructed like the first one you saw.

Note 3

Unlike the usual figure-ground pictures, the information in this picture is in both the background (white) and the foreground (black). To see what it is, look at both the black shapes and at the white "spaces."

Note 4

Here's another copy of the picture puzzle for you to draw on. Use a light pencil to draw around some of the black and white shapes to see whether you can discover what the picture is.

Note 5

Cover the list of words below so that only the first word shows. See whether that gives you enough information to figure out the picture. If not, uncover the second word to see whether you have enough information then. Proceed down the list until you see what the picture is. Note: don't worry if you don't see it even after you read all the words; you're not alone—roughly 10% of people never see it, even with all kinds of clues!

Hat

Legs

Running

Tail

Hooves

Man

Cowboy

Horse

Note 6

Here's the "answer" to the puzzle picture. Notice how the cowboy and horse in the original picture are depicted by both the black forms and the white "spaces."

Note 7

Here's the "answer" to the second picture.

2

What Is Learner Centered From an Evidence-Based Perspective?

Think back for a moment to the beginning of Chapter 1, where we asked you to reflect on how you approached figuring out the image in the puzzle picture. Our approach there was to invite you to engage with us in the process of learning something new (unless you're one of the 10% of people who saw the image right away). Rather than assuming that all readers should approach the problem in a similar way, we focused on you as an individual reader and learner with extensive knowledge about how you learn, which strategies work best for you, which don't, and whether you were even interested enough to play the game of figuring out the "answer" to the puzzle. Our purpose was—and is—to encourage you to reflect on your learning processes in such a way that your interest and curiosity are continually stimulated and energized as you continue your journey of lifelong learning, continuous change, and improvement.

What Does "Learner Centered" Mean?

What do we mean by "learner centered?" Our focus on you as an individual learner and the processes we hope you engage in as you read this book represents half of what we mean by "learner centered." Each of us brings a unique combination of factors to any learning situation: heredity; temperament; experiential history; beliefs, values, and perspectives; talents; interests; capacities; and needs, to name just a few. Your approach to solving the puzzle picture in Chapter 1 was influenced by all these factors, whether or not you were conscious of their effect.

The other half of what we mean by "learner centered" is a focus on the "best available knowledge about learning and how it occurs and about teaching practices that are most effective in promoting the highest levels of motivation and achievement" (McCombs &

Whisler, 1997, p. 9). You will recall our discussion in Chapter 1 of the evidence showing that the most highly motivated learning of all, self-motivated learning, occurs only when learners possess (1) choice and control about how, what, and when to learn and (2) choice and control over what they want to achieve.

Putting both parts of the concept together, "learner centered" can be understood as the combination of a focus on individual learners with a focus on the best available knowledge we have about learning and the teaching practices that support learning for all teachers and students alike.

What Is "Learner Centered"?

"Learner centered" is the perspective that combines a focus on individual learners— their heredity, experiences, perspectives, backgrounds, talents, interests, capacities, and needs—with a focus on the best available knowledge about learning and how it occurs and about teaching practices that promote the highest levels of motivation, learning, and achievement for all learners. This dual focus then informs and drives educational decision making. "Learner centered" is a reflection in practice of the Learner-Centered Psychological Principles in the programs, practices, policies, and people that support learning for all.

SOURCE: McCombs and Whisler (1997).

Consider how the term "learner centered" fits into the context of your experiences with professional development. For some educators, it refers to learning new beliefs and new visions of practice that are responsive to and respectful of the diverse needs of students and teachers as learners (Darling-Hammond, 1996; Sparks & Hirsh, 1997). From this perspective, "learner centered" means that professional development strategies must support diverse learner needs and perspectives, provide time for critical reflection, and offer opportunities for teachers to re-create their practices and beliefs about students and instruction. It also means that teachers, like the students they teach, must be actively involved in their own learning processes in a collaborative process with other educators, teachers, and experts from higher education and the community. This view of "learner centered," which is based on a substantial body of research evidence, constitutes a true paradigm shift, a transformation that is badly needed for professional development. To challenge misconceptions about learners and learning, to identify common elements of successful programs, and to create better ways to prepare quality teachers all require a shift to this new paradigm and a deeper understanding of current research about learning and instructional practices (e.g., Feistritzer, 1999; Putnam & Borko, 2000).

Perhaps more critical than how a learner-centered approach can positively influence professional development, however, is the effect of learner-centered practices in classrooms and schools. The research on learner-centered practices provides a clear foundation for creating positive learning contexts and communities at the classroom and school levels so that the likelihood of success is increased for teachers and students alike.

Our experience has been that putting the Learner-Centered Model into practice results in increased motivation, learning, and academic achievement for a much larger number of students, including many who are currently underachieving or dropping out. Utilizing the Learner-Centered Model in your own classroom, you will automatically discover the unique learner characteristics of your students. In addition, you will learn the teaching and learning characteristics of teachers who are the most successful in providing the learning contexts and experiences that motivate their students to the highest achievement levels and the pursuit of learning beyond school and throughout their lifetimes.

In spite of clear evidence about the effectiveness of learner-centered teaching, the use of evidence-based, learner-centered principles and practices is not yet widespread. Instead, the well-publicized focus of current efforts has been on cognitive outcomes and academic achievement of content standards. However, as you are undoubtedly aware, this focus has not led to desired increases in student achievement in the majority of American schools, nor has it stemmed the ever-increasing dropout rates endemic to many schools. Further, engagement in school learning and academic achievement are declining for large numbers of school-age children. Social problems, including school dropout, are on the rise, along with associated problems of absenteeism, disruptive behaviors, and even school violence. As currently structured, the educational system is obviously out of balance. We believe that encouraging the widespread use of learner-centered practices can restore faith in schools as places where students are encouraged to learn meaningful and relevant skills that will serve them well as active participants when they take their place in society.

Seeing the Big Picture: Education as a Complex Living System

Increasingly, those concerned with education and educational reform are looking at learning and change as complex living systems (e.g., Lemke, 2002; Wheatley, 1999a, 1999b). The living systems model provides the perspective necessary for developing instruction for both learning and learners. Viewed from the perspective of living systems, the Learner-Centered Model (LCM) and associated Learner-Centered Principles (LCPs) define how learners function, how they learn and develop, and what best supports the natural lifelong learning processes that lead to continued development and change. The LCPs, described in detail below, serve as a foundation and framework for further research and development and for creating the kinds of caring learning communities that support all learners (cf. Fullan, 1997, 2000).

Researchers and educators working in the area of living systems and systemic change agree that negative, fear-based approaches do not work (e.g., Wheatley, 1999a; Wheatley & Kellner-Rogers, 1998). What does work are approaches that are restorative and strength based and that focus on positive growth and development. Such approaches are predicated on the view that all people are connected and that relationships and networks are the natural form of organization in life—life consists of interconnected and interdependent webs of relationships.

Another way to understand learning as a living system is to view it as an ecology (Deakin Crick & McCombs, in press). What this means is that for learning to be most effective, the climate of the classroom must support the factors inside and outside the learner that influence learning. For example, the way learners view themselves and the quality of the relationships associated with their learning (i.e., with their teachers, peers, materials, scheduling, curriculum, etc.) all contribute to how engaged they are in the learning process as well as to the quality of their learning outcomes. If learners are worried about their competence or ability to succeed in learning activities, learning outcomes suffer. Similarly, if learners are concerned about how well they fit in and whether their teachers care about them, the quality of their learning will suffer. Work by Deakin Crick and McCombs (in press) in Great Britain on the ecology of learning and what best develops students' learning power has shown that learner-centered classrooms and schools contribute to a number of positive student learning outcomes as compared with non-learner-centered classrooms and schools. Deakin Crick and McCombs's research in three elementary and two secondary schools showed that the positive student learning outcomes include not only higher student classroom achievement, but higher active learning skills, higher intrinsic learning goals, higher motivation to learn, higher confidence in their ability to be successful learners, and higher lifelong learning skills in seven areas:

1. changing and learning as a learner,

2. critical curiosity,

3. meaning making,

4. creativity,

5. learning relationships,

6. strategic awareness, and

7. resilience.

In Chapters 4 and 5, we will talk more about these important outcomes and specific learner-centered strategies that can be used to achieve them.

Systems thinking has important implications for how educational systems are designed because it helps everyone involved to understand the power of systems to change processes such as learning and teaching (Sparks & Hirsh, 1997). Applying systems thinking within *a living systems perspective,* Wheatley (1999b) points out that no behavior can be understood in isolation from the whole of the system and its interdependent dynamics across time. Describing a principle from biology, she says that to make a system stronger, stronger relationships must be created with *itself.* This means that the nature of humans as living systems is to *learn more about themselves from themselves* through self-discovery and the creation of new relationships. Learning, change, and continuous improvement are the primary processes by which individuals within living systems grow. These growth processes also reflect the relational, interdependent, connected nature of human beings. The research on learner-centered models and approaches shows clearly that human learning flourishes when it is based on these natural growth processes.

Schools and education in general can be viewed from the framework of living systems composed of three domains: technical, organizational, and personal (see Figure 2.1; McCombs, 2000a, 2001; McCombs & Whisler, 1997).

Figure 2.1   Conceptual Framework: Domains of Living Systems as Levels of Interventions Related to Systemic Research on Engagement

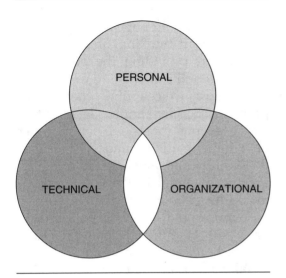

McCombs (1999a, 2000a, 2001) has argued that most recent reform efforts have tended to focus on changes in the technical (curriculum, standards, assessment, instruction) or organizational (decision making, management structures, time allocations) domain to the exclusion of the personal domain (individual and collective beliefs, relationships, motivation, learning). The resulting imbalance has led to unhealthy system functioning as well as teachers and students feeling stressed, alienated, and demoralized.

People who see schools as living systems focus on the learner and the personal domain (Wheatley & Kellner-Rogers, 1998). As people in living systems such as education are given more opportunities to be creatively involved in how their work gets done, standards of functioning are not imposed or mandated from outside, but rather, these standards, measures, values, organizational structures, and plans come from within through an ongoing dialogue in which people—teachers, students, administrators, families—share perceptions, seek out a diversity of interpretations, and agree on what needs to be done. Through the process of learning and change, the people engaged in the dialogue call upon the best evidence available—that is, research-validated principles—as guides for determining what will work well in the current situation or context. In this way, the system, based on the learner-centered model, takes care of self, others, and the place (Wheatley & Kellner-Rogers, 1998). Through its focus on learners and learning, which shifts emphasis from the individual as a receptacle to be filled with information to relationships with others as a means for creating learning communities, personal and system supports emerge that facilitate and support everyone's learning. In learner-centered systems, where every learner matters, challenging and caring communities of learners emerge to create new and unique learning challenges that benefit everyone involved. The new cultures that emerge restore the joy of teaching and learning.

Domains of Schools as Living Systems

In any system that supports basic human needs, such as schools supporting the need for learning, people are at the heart of the system, which serves to support positive learning, growth, and development for all learners, teachers, and schools (Wheatley, 1999b). The domains of school as a living system (shown in Figure 2.1 above) are

- personal—the personal, motivational, and interpersonal needs of those in the system (e.g., students, teachers, administrators, parents);
- technical—the content standards, curriculum structures, instructional approaches, and assessment strategies that promote learning and achievement; and
- organizational—the management structures and policies that support the personal and technical domains and, ultimately, motivation, learning, and achievement for all students.

Thinking about schools as living systems has helped teachers and other educators develop new metaphors for thinking about and improving schools and schooling. For example, one metaphor that has emerged from the living systems perspective is to look at schools and classrooms from an ecological point of view in which learning is defined by the relationships between learners (including teachers) and their environments. Seen as an ecological system, schools are communities that prepare all learners for lifelong learning by setting up the conditions and contexts for learning for life through implementing the LCPs. These practices can transform schools into communities of learners (another metaphor emanating from the living systems perspective) in a learning partnership that is part of a continuous learning and improvement process.

Thomas J. Sergiovanni, a nationally recognized writer on educational leadership, has analyzed how schools operate successfully and how leaders lead most effectively. One of his conclusions is that metaphors such as the ones we are describing carry practical importance because they give rise to human concerns and emotions, including hope and faith (Sergiovanni, 2004). Viewing schools as communities provides a means for placing hope at its core, promoting clear thinking and informed action and providing the encouragement needed to close the achievement gap as well as solve other serious problems. Sergiovanni has learned that when people in school communities have hope that is grounded in realistic possibilities and connected to recognizing the potential in the community—including people *and* situations—they are empowered to create policies and programs rather than react to externally dictated policies and programs.

Taking Sergiovanni's results a step further, we believe that faith, which is integral to hope, provides commitment to a cause and strong belief in a set of ideas, for example,

- all students can succeed and take responsibility for their own learning,
- schools can transform themselves into caring learning communities,
- all parents can be effective partners, and
- all teachers can become leaders.

When members of the school community focus on developing a community of hope, leadership is elevated to the level of moral action. However, the success of the community depends to a large extent on turning hope into reality, which means

- specifying goals,
- specifying pathways or routes to realize goals,

- identifying obstacles,
- making a commitment to realize goals, and
- strengthening beliefs that success is possible.

The Learner-Centered Model

To give you a picture of how the LCPs connect all the people involved with the educational system, we've developed several figures and diagrams that show the various components of the educational system, based on the LCPs that comprise the Learner-Centered Model (LCM). In the LCM, each component is part of a complex, living system. Each of these diagrams illustrates one or more aspects of

engagement, with learners connected in caring learning communities.

Recall that Figure 2.1 shows schools—complex living systems—as having personal, technical, and organizational domains. Research evidence confirms that when these three domains are in balance and based on an alignment of personal beliefs, values, and philosophies, more effective teaching and learning occurs (Fullan, 2001).

Figure 2.2 illustrates the central role of people in establishing the personal and system climate for schooling, along with a visualization of the reciprocal role of learning and change in living systems. As people explore their fundamental beliefs, assumptions, values, attitudes, and learning together, they are inspired to make both personal and

Figure 2.2   Belief and the Change Process

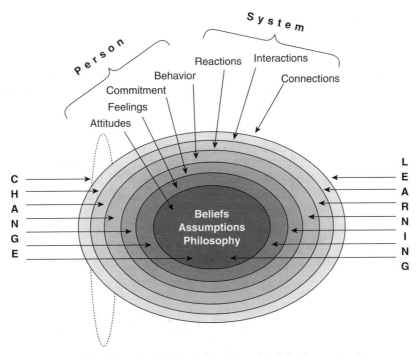

Constituencies: Students, Teachers, Administrators, Parents, Business and Community Members

Figure 2.3   Elements of Living Systems

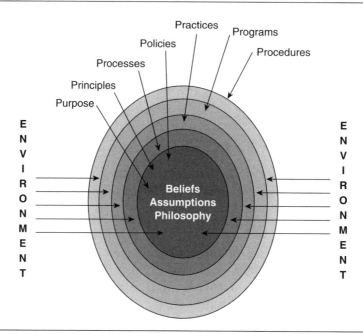

systemic changes by creating new meanings, learning relationships, and ways of interacting that in turn influence each individual learner within the system.

Figure 2.3 shows how the shared beliefs, assumptions, values, and philosophies depicted in Figure 2.2 result in the purpose, principles, processes, policies, practices, programs, and procedures that are developed and implemented in the system. The "environment" refers to the overall educational context—school, classroom, and even family influences. What arises from everyone beginning with an exploration of beliefs, values, and so on—reflected in all the "P" words—is the overall vision and processes for the school.

Figure 2.4 of the LCM shows the role of the LCP domains (cognitive and metacognitive, motivational and affective, social and developmental,

individual differences) in providing the scientific basis for holistic instructional practices. The figure illustrates that the LCM, resting on the foundation created by the 14 LCPs, focuses on the learner as the core of instructional decision making. This is not to say that the LCM disregards the importance of the processes of learning or the acquisition of knowledge and content. Through its emphasis on the importance of understanding each learner's unique characteristics and needs, as well as the particular qualities of the learning communities that emerge, the LCM incorporates the best qualities of both learner-centered (child-centered) approaches and approaches that emphasize knowledge acquisition and content. The major shift—and what we believe is the power of the LCM to put the educational system back in balance—is that the LCM begins the process of instructional decision

Figure 2.4   Learner-Centered Model: A Holistic Perspective

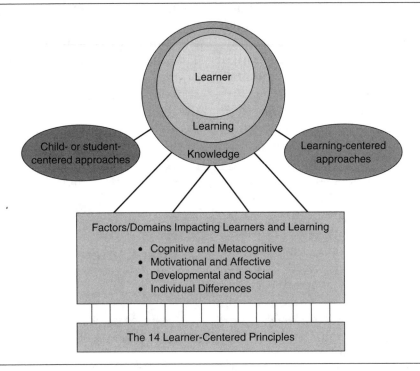

making with knowing individual learners and building classroom learning communities. When teachers have knowledge of individual learners and their needs, strengths, and interests—surrounded by a strong knowledge base in learning and what best promotes learning in diverse learners—they can then focus on teaching the desired knowledge, content, and skills. If learning or knowledge is in the center, students know that the system isn't about them, and they begin to feel alienated and disengaged. The LCM puts the system back into balance.

In a nutshell, Figure 2.4 emphasizes that in the overall educational system and in the classroom in particular, decisions about programming, personnel, and instructional practices begin with knowledge of individuals as learners. The model indicates how decisions

regarding schooling operate with the best available research knowledge on what constitutes learning and how it is best supported in all content or knowledge domains, for example, literacy, numeracy, scientific understanding, problem-solving and critical thinking skills, social and emotional skills.

The LCM provides a framework for sharing power and control with students and for building the positive relationships and connections essential to high motivation and achievement. The LCM creates a positive school and classroom climate by

- automatically engaging students and other people associated with the school community,
- discouraging negative social behaviors, and
- enhancing personal development.

Unlike many programs, however, the LCM provides an overall framework for aligning existing programs and practices. The underlying LCPs apply to all learners of all ages and settings and define learning and motivation as natural processes that flourish given the right conditions and contexts.

What a learner-centered perspective and model help us understand is that individual learners, young and old, students and teachers—like all human beings—bring with them a complex array of unique viewpoints, needs, capacities, and strengths. At the same time, they share certain fundamental qualities. The inherent need to grow, live, and develop in a positive direction, for example, is common to all learners (McCombs & Whisler, 1997).

When translated into practice, the LCM consists of a variety of materials, guided reflection, and assessment tools that support teacher effectiveness and change at the individual and school levels. The LCM, which is based on the LCPs, includes staff development workshops and videos demonstrating learner-centered practices in diverse school settings. As an additional support for teachers changing their practices, McCombs, in collaboration with colleagues (McCombs, 2001, 2003b; McCombs & Lauer, 1997, 1998; McCombs & Whisler, 1997), developed a set of self-assessment and reflection tools for K–20 teachers: the Assessment of Learner-Centered Practices (ALCP). The ALCP includes surveys for teachers, students, and administrators that facilitate reflection and a willingness to change instructional practices. The teacher survey offers an opportunity for teachers to discover how our personal beliefs about learners, learning, and teaching might agree or disagree with the knowledge base underlying the Learner-Centered Principles.

To see how the survey works, take the mini-assessment in Activity 2.1. The mini-assessment, a short form of the ALCP Teacher Beliefs Survey, contains 15 of the items that are on the long form. After you finish the mini-assessment, compare your score with the interpretation rubric to see how your beliefs compare with those that are considered learner centered.

What Are the Learner-Centered Principles?

Research-Validated Learner-Centered Principles

The research-validated Principles show educators how to help students know their worth, their competencies, their abilities to choose and be in control, and their role in generating the will to learn. An understanding of the research on learning and learners discloses that all children are gifted and talented in different ways. The systems that educate all school-age children have a responsibility to foster beliefs, learning environments, and learning communities that benefit all learners and value their diversity.

SOURCE: McCombs (in press).

The LCPs shown in Table 2.1 serve as the foundation for the Learner-Centered Model (LCM) we described in the previous section. Based on years of research into learners and learning, the LCPs have been adopted by the American Psychological Association as a definition of the psychological principles with the greatest effect on learners and learning (APA Work Group of the Board of Educational Affairs, 1997).[1] The 14 LCPs define what we know about learning and learners as a result of research into both. Many of these principles are consistent with recent discoveries from psychology relating to positive youth development and prevention interventions (Larson, 2000; Seligman & Csikszentmihalyi, 2000). These discoveries highlight the natural learning and motivation of all youth and the power of interventions that empower youth to take responsibility for their own positive self-development.

The LCPs are organized into four categories, or domains, of factors that affect learners and learning in a variety of ways, as shown in Table 2.1. The four domains holistically describe the factors that must be attended to in facilitating learning for all learners.

The LCPs apply to all learners, in and out of school, young and old. Research with the ALCP for teachers and students from K–12 and in college classrooms confirms that what defines "learner-centeredness" is not solely a function of particular instructional practices or programs (McCombs & Lauer, 1997; McCombs & Whisler, 1997). Rather, learner-centeredness is a complex interaction of the programs, practices, policies, and people as perceived by the individual learners (McCombs, 2003a, 2004b). The LCPs serve as the foundation for determining how to use and evaluate programs and practices that provide instruction, curricula, and personnel to enhance the teaching and learning process.

Research underlying the LCPs confirms that learning is nonlinear, recursive, continuous, complex, relational, and natural in humans. The evidence also shows that learning is enhanced in contexts in which learners have supportive relationships, have a sense of ownership and control over the learning process, and can learn with and from each other in safe and trusting learning environments (McCombs, 2003b, 2004a). In much of the traditional K–20 educational system, however, learners often feel isolated, and learning is often simplistic and rote, with a focus on linear teaching of knowledge and skill standards. The key processes involved in developing learner-centered principles and practices are

- building ways to meet learner needs for interpersonal relationships and connections;
- finding strategies that acknowledge individual differences and the diversity of learner needs, abilities, and interests;
- tailoring strategies to differing learner needs for personal control and choice; and
- assessing the efficacy of instructional practices to meet diverse and emerging individual learner and learning community needs.

As an overriding principle, it is necessary to look for not only the match or mismatch of instructional practices with learning principles, but also their match or mismatch with learners and their diverse needs. A balance of personal and technical supports can then be provided with a variety of learning opportunities, content requirements, and communities of learning.

When the 14 LCPs are applied to schools and classrooms, they address each of the four learning domains. The resulting learner-centered framework provides a systemic approach to content, context, assessment, and individual

(Text continued on page 32)

The Assessment of Learner-Centered Practices (ALCP)
Teacher Beliefs Survey 1 (Short Form)©

A Learner-Centered Self-Assessment for Teachers: In the discussion so far, we have talked about how our personal beliefs about learners, learning, and teaching might agree or disagree with the knowledge base as represented in the *Learner-Centered Psychological Principles*. The following self-assessment gives you an opportunity to look at your beliefs and compare them with what would be considered "learner-centered" beliefs in the Scoring Guide.

Directions: Please read each of the statements below. Decide to what extent you agree or disagree with each statement. Circle the letter that best matches your choice for each statement. Go with your first judgment and do not spend too much time on any one statement. PLEASE ANSWER EVERY QUESTION.

A = Strongly Disagree • B = Somewhat Disagree • C = Somewhat Agree • D = Strongly Agree

		Strongly Disagree	Somewhat Disagree	Somewhat Agree	Strongly Agree
1.	In order to maximize learning, I need to help students feel comfortable in discussing their feelings and beliefs.	A	B	C	D
2.	It's impossible to work with students who refuse to learn.	A	B	C	D
3.	No matter how badly a teacher feels, s/he has a responsibility to not let students know about those feelings.	A	B	C	D
4.	Taking the time to create caring relationships with my students is the most important element for student achievement.	A	B	C	D
5.	I can't help feeling upset and inadequate when dealing with difficult students.	A	B	C	D
6.	If I don't prompt and provide direction for student questions, they won't get the right answer.	A	B	C	D
7.	I can help students who are uninterested in learning get in touch with their natural motivation to learn.	A	B	C	D
8.	No matter what I do or how hard I try, there are some students who are unreachable.	A	B	C	D

		Strongly Disagree	Somewhat Disagree	Somewhat Agree	Strongly Agree
9.	Knowledge of the subject area is the most important part of being an effective teacher.	A	B	C	D
10.	Students will be more motivated to learn if teachers get to know them at a personal level.	A	B	C	D
11.	Innate ability is fairly fixed, and some children just can't learn as well as others.	A	B	C	D
12.	One of the most important things I can teach students is how to follow rules and to do what is expected of them in the classroom.	A	B	C	D
13.	Being willing to share who I am as a person with my students facilitates learning more than being an authority figure.	A	B	C	D
14.	Even with feedback, some students just can't figure out their mistakes.	A	B	C	D
15.	I am responsible for what my students learn and how they learn.	A	B	C	D

Scoring

A responses = 1 point   B responses = 2 points   C responses = 3 points   D responses = 4 points

Add your scores from items 1, 4, 7, 10, & 13   Total _____   Divide by 5 _____

Add your scores from items 2, 5, 8, 11, & 14   Total _____   Divide by 5 _____

Add your scores from items 3, 6, 9, 12, & 15   Total _____   Divide by 5 _____

Turn to page 28 to see how your scores compare with the learner-centered beliefs associated with the Learner-Centered Principles.

ACTIVITY 2.1

Interpretation Assessment of Learner-Centered Practices (ALCP) Teacher Beliefs Survey (Short Form)©

The Teachers Beliefs Survey Short Form has 15 of the 35 items that are on the long form. These 15 items comprise three subscales with 5 items on each scale. When you scored your responses on the Teacher Beliefs Survey Short Form, you added the total of your scores for each of the three subtests and divided by 5 to arrive at your average score for each subscale.

To get an idea of how your beliefs compare with what is considered learner centered, compare your scores on the three subscales with the rubric provided below.

Scale 1   **Learner-Centered Beliefs about Learners, Learning, and Teaching**

Items 1, 4, 7, 10, 13   My Score _____ (total ÷ 5)   Rubric Score ____3.2____

Scale 2   **Non-Learner-Centered Beliefs about Learners**

Items 2, 5, 8, 11, 14   My Score _____ (total ÷ 5)   Rubric Score ____2.3____

Scale 3   **Non-Learner-Centered Beliefs about Learning and Teaching**

Items 3, 6, 9, 12, 15   My Score _____ (total ÷ 5)   Rubric Score ____2.4____

SCORING KEY:

ASSESSMENT OF LEARNER-CENTERED PRACTICES (ALCP)

Teacher Beliefs Survey (Short Form)©

DIRECTIONS:

The short form of the ALCP Teacher Beliefs Survey has 15 of 35 items that are on the long form. These 15 items comprise three subscales with 5 items on each scale.

Use the following items to group your scores on the three subscales. Give yourself a 4 for all D responses, a 3 for all C responses, a 2 for all B responses, and a 1 for all A responses.

Scale 1:   Learner-Centered Beliefs about Learners, Learning, and Teaching

> Items 1, 4, 7, 10, 13   Total Score = _____
>
> Total Divided by 5 = _____

Scale 2:   Non Learner-Centered Beliefs about Learners

> Items 2, 5, 8, 11, 14   Total Score = _____
>
> Total Divided by 5 = _____

Scale 3:   Non Learner-Centered Beliefs about Learning and Teaching

> Items 3, 6, 9, 12, 15   Total Score = _____
>
> Total Divided by 5 = _____

Comparing your score to the Learner-Centered Rubric for each subscale:

	My Score	Rubric
Learner-Centered Beliefs about Learners, Learning, and Teaching	_____	3.2
Non Learner-Centered Beliefs about Learners	_____	2.3
Non Learner-Centered Beliefs about Learning and Teaching	_____	2.4

Table 2.1   The Four Domains of Learner-Centered Principles

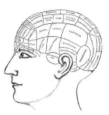

Cognitive and Metacognitive Factors

1. Nature of the learning process. Learning is a natural process of pursuing personally meaningful goals. Learning is an active, goal-oriented, and self-regulating process of discovering and constructing meaning from individual learner's experierience and information. Successful learners assume personal responsibility for their own learning.

2. Goals of the learning process. The successful learner seeks to create meaningful, coherent representations of knowledge. Over time and with support, students' understandng can be refined so that they reach their long-term goals. Educators can support students' creating personally meaningful learning goals that are consistent with their personal aspirations and interests, as well as with educational goals.

3. Construction of knowledge. The successful learner can link new information with existing and future knowledge in meaningful ways. This linking integrates students' prior knowledge and understanding with new knowledge that can be used effectively in new tasks and transferred readily to new situations.

4. Strategic thinking. The sucessful learner can create and use various thinking and reasoning strategies to achieve complex learning goals and apply their knowledge to novel situations.

5. Thinking about thinking. The successful learner can develop higher order strategies for selecting and monitoring mental operations, which facilitates creative and critical thinking. The learner develops metacognitive approaches for dealing with problems.

6. Context of learning. Learning is influenced by a variety of factors, including culture, technology, and instructional practices. Technologies and practices must be appropriate for individual learners in order to provide a nurturing context for learning.

Motivational and Affective Factors

7. Motivational and emotional influences on learning. What a learner learns—and how much—depends on her/his motivation. Motivation to learn is influenced by the individual's emotional states, beliefs, interests and goals, and habits of thinking.

8. Intrinsic motivation to learn. Individuals are naturally creative and curious, utilize higher-order thinking, and enjoy learning, all of which contribute to motivation to learn. Intrinsic motivation to learn is stimulated by tasks that present optimal novelty and difficulty, are relevant to students' personal interests, reflect real-world situations, and provide for personal choice and control.

9. Effects of motivation on effort. Without the motivation to engage in the effort required to acquire complex knowledge and skills, students' willingness is unlikely. Teachers can promote student effort through purposeful learning activities that are guided by practices that enhance positive emotions, and by methods that increase the learner's perception that a task is interesting and personally relevant.

Developmental and Social Factors

10. Developmental influence on learning. Individuals experience different opportunities and situations as they develop physically, intellectually, emotionally, and socially. Learning is most effective when these individual developmental differences among learners are taken into account.

11. Social influences on learning. Social interactions, interpersonal relations, and communication with others all influence learning. Learning is enhanced when learners have opportunities to engage in interactive and collaborative instructional contexts.

Individual Differences Factors

12. Individual differences in learning. Learners have different strategies, approaches, capabilities, and preferences for learning, each a function of prior experience and heredity. The degree to which these differences are accepted and adapted to is directly correlated with successful learning.

13. Learning and diversity. The most effective learning occurs when learners perceive that their linguistic, cultural, and social backgrounds are taken into account.

14. Standards and assessment. Effective learning takes place when learners are challenged to work toward appropriately high goals and when ongoing assessment is used to provide valuable feedback to learners about their understanding, knowledge, and skills.

SOURCE: Adapted from American Psychological Association. (1997). *Learner-centered psychological principles: A framework for school reform and redesign.* Washington, DC: APA, and McCombs, B.L., & Whisler, J.S. (1997). *The learner-centered classroom and school: Strategies for increasing student motivation and achievement.* San Francisco: Jossey-Bass. Used by permission.

learner needs. In addition, basing educational practices on the LCM and its associated LCPs provides a means for transforming education. The role of teacher changes to that of co-learner and contributor to the social and interpersonal development of students. In partnership with their teachers, students become responsible for their learning and participate equally in determining what, how, and when they learn. The learner-centered framework adds a constant reminder that the human element cannot be left out of even the most advanced educational systems, including technology-supported networked learning communities (cf. McCombs & Vakili, 2005).

Factors Affecting Learners and Learning

Taken together, the four domains of the LCPs offer a holistic way of looking at how the LCPs combine and interact to influence learners and learning. That is, the research on which the LCPs are based shows that they "clump together" into the four domains as follows:

- Cognitive and metacognitive—what the intellectual capacities of learners are and how they facilitate the learning process.
- Motivational and affective—the roles played by motivation and emotions in learning.
- Developmental and social—the influence of various aspects of learner development and the importance of interpersonal interactions in learning and change.
- Individual differences—how individual differences influence learning; how teachers, students, and administrators adapt to learning

diversity; and how standards and assessment can best support individual differences in learners.

Each of the four domains affects each learner in a unique way, as does the dynamic resulting from the interaction of the four domains.

What's Next?

In Chapter 3, we take a look at what teachers and students tell us about learner-centered practices. We describe how the LCPs are translated into practice and their relationship to testing and accountability and what they mean for teaching and learning. We tell you the characteristics of effective teachers and how those characteristics reflect the LCPs. We report on what students say about effective teaching and tell you about international evidence regarding students as meaningful partners in learning. In the final sections of the chapter, we describe some strategies you can use to honor students' voices, and we guide you through a reflection designed to begin the process of learning more about and with your students.

Note

1. The research that is summarized in the APA *Principles* derives from many fields, including psychology, education, sociology, and brain research. Research documentation can be found in Alexander and Murphy (1998); Combs, Miser, and Whitaker (1999); Ford (1992); Kanfer and McCombs (2000); Lambert and McCombs (1998); McCombs (2001); McCombs and Whisler (1997); Marshall (1992, 1996); and Perry and Weinstein (1998). Copies of the *Principles* may be obtained by e-mailing education@apa.org.

3

What Teachers and Students Tell Us About Learner-Centered Practices

Teachers and students have a long history of knowing what works and what does not work in schools. Both say learner-centered practices work, and they work well.

What Teachers Have Recognized About the LCPs

As early drafts of the Learner-Centered Principles (LCPs) were disseminated at all levels of the PreK–20 system (and beyond), experienced teachers recognized from their own practice the validity of the principles. They recognized the "truths" represented in the principles—truths about human nature, learning, motivation, and development. They recognized that knowing, believing, and practicing in ways that reflect these principles had allowed them to make a difference in the lives and learning potential of their individual students from diverse social, ethnic, and racial groups.

Experienced teachers were heartened to see that the evidence-based (i.e., research-validated) principles define learners of all ages as individuals with minds, emotions, and personal, developmental, social, cultural, and other individual differences and needs that must be addressed in educational contexts. In other words, the LCPs begin with the premise that learners are viewed holistically, as human beings, rather than as isolated clumps of characteristics or attributes, or worse, problems to be dealt with or removed.

Translating the LCPs Into Practice

The LCPs, though we have presented and described them individually and as components of the four domains, are meant to be understood and applied as an entity. Instructional practices based on these principles incorporate all of them, albeit weighted differently according to the unique needs and characteristics of each learner and learning environment.

Instructional practices derived from individual principles run the risk of leading to learners feeling personally isolated, excluded, and/or alienated, issues which arise when learners do not feel respected and cared about as unique individuals. A central understanding emerging from the LCPs is that for educational systems to serve the needs of *all learners*, these systems must

- focus on the individual learner,
- reflect an understanding of the learning process, and
- address the essential knowledge and skills to be learned.

Learner-centered really means that you look at what the needs of an individual are and that you center the curriculum around where the students are, around their past experience, so that you can help them construct new meaning from new experiences. (Superintendent in a large Midwestern high school)

The LCPs, Testing, and Accountability

The American Psychological Association (APA) adopted the LCPs in 1997 largely as a response to what the APA considered ill-informed decisions being made based on the *Nation at Risk* report that was published in 1983 (The National Commission on Excellence in Education, 1983). You may know that

Nation at Risk concluded that student achievement in the U.S. showed an alarming decline, especially in comparison with other countries, such as Japan. As a consequence, political leaders began responding with a call for greater accountability and standards for education. In 1989, the National Governors' Association was asked to meet with presidential committees to formulate the National Education Goals, which later became Goals 2000 and then the America 2000 national education goals ("Goals 2000," 1994). Discussions began about the need for national standards in all academic disciplines, with much talk about the need for national and state assessments that could provide greater levels of accountability for student achievement of rigorous academic standards.

However, the APA was concerned that the push toward testing and accountability was not informed by evidence regarding what best supports and fosters learning. The members of the APA Task Force (1993) working on the LCPs believed that psychology, as a scientific field that has studied learning for over 100 years, had a responsibility to clearly present to educators and policy makers its accumulated and research-validated knowledge base about learning and learners. Members of the Task Force were committed to exploring how school reform could be informed by contributions of psychology that help us understand the learner in different learning contexts.

When work on the LCPs began, no one knew what the final product would look like or what it would be called. The Task Force saw it as a "living document" that would be revised and reissued as more was learned about learning, motivation, development, and individual differences that must be addressed to achieve optimal learning for all. The LCPs document is now in its second iteration and continues to be widely disseminated to educators and researchers in the United States and abroad (APA Work Group of the Board of Educational Affairs, 1997).

A number of researchers (Amrein & Berliner, 2003; Neill, 2003) are increasingly arguing that high-stakes testing will not improve schools. Rather, just the opposite seems to be the case. Research is consistently showing that a focus on high-stakes testing narrows curriculum and "dumbs down" instruction. As a result, students disengage, and many drop out mentally, emotionally, or physically. Worse, many schools are induced to push students out, increase grade retention, force many teachers to leave, and impede real and needed improvements. The bottom line is that those students most in need of quality schools are those the most hurt. In more than a decade of research, we have learned that those states without high-stakes tests had (a) more improvement in average scores on the National Assessment of Educational Progress (NAEP) than states with such tests, (b) improvement at a faster rate on a variety of standardized tests, and (c) higher motivation and lower dropout rates (Amrein & Berliner, 2003). In fact, researchers have found that the stakes attached to performance on these tests lead to less intrinsic motivation to learn and lower levels of critical thinking (Neill, 2003). In environments that focus on student performance on high-stakes tests, teachers are less inclined to encourage students to explore concepts and subjects of interest to them, thus obstructing students' paths to becoming lifelong, self-directed learners.

Further, high-stakes testing does not adequately deal with low-income and non-English-speaking students and can lead to teaching to the test and inflated and/or misleading test scores. More effective approaches include engaging students in self-evaluation and meaningful feedback in the form of formative assessment that provides them with information on their learning progress, particularly benefiting low achievers.

For schools and districts with whom the LCPs have been widely shared, teaching practices are achieving a more balanced approach that encourages high student learning and achievement while also promoting learner-centered approaches. These learner-centered approaches, recognized in many of the nation's most excellent schools, reflect both conventional and scientific wisdom that can lead to effective schooling and to positive mental health and productivity of our nation's children, their teachers, and the systems that serve them. They create a new vision of schooling.

What Do the LCPs Mean for Teaching and Learning?

Putting learners first is at the heart of learner-centered teaching. It requires knowing individual learners and providing a safe and nurturing context before the job of teaching can begin. Learner-centered teaching starts with teachers who understand that they must find ways to know their individual students. Teachers who engage in learner-centered teaching also understand that not only is learning a natural lifelong process, but motivation to learn is also natural when the learning context is supportive. Learner-centered teachers know that all students *are learners* (not just capable of learning) and that they want to learn in order to make sense of and contribute to the world around them. If these teachers see evidence that students are not learning or do not seem motivated to learn, they do not blame the students (or their parents). They look at what is not happening in the teaching and learning process or in the learning context that results in these natural processes being blocked.

Underlying learner-centered teaching is an understanding of the basic human needs for control, competence, and belonging. Various researchers (Battistich, Soloman, Watson, & Schaps, 1997; Glasser, 1990) have demonstrated students' fundamental need to develop a sense of belonging as a member of their class and school community. Ryan and Deci (2000) maintain that nurturing competence, autonomy, and relatedness reduces alienation and enhances motivation and engagement in any age population.

Learner-centered teachers know that listening to students provides a blueprint for finding the most effective practices and for engaging students' voices in the process of learning. They encourage students to talk about how they would meet their own learning needs, satisfy their natural curiosity, and make sense of things.

What the Evidence Shows: Characteristics of Effective Teachers

In looking at the evidence for learner-centered practices, it is important to begin with an understanding of schools and classrooms as part of a comprehensive system set up to support learning. Educational systems can have a variety of goals, but to support learning, the focus must start with learners.

The LCPs we've been describing rest on a strong evidence base, thus providing the platform for evidence-based practice. Specifically, research to date demonstrates that learning is enhanced in contexts where learners have supportive relationships, have a sense of ownership and control over the learning process, and can learn with and from each other in safe and trusting learning environments (McCombs, 2003a, 2004b).

The research findings in the box on the next page support the case for learner-centered practices, particularly given the current emphasis on content standards and accountability through student testing.

As the research shown in the box illustrates, learner-centered teaching rests on the belief that learning is a partnership between teachers and students. This partnership is based on evidence that practices promoting positive relationships and honoring student voices are critical for high student motivation and achievement. Learner-centered teaching is also defined by student perceptions that teachers care and want to listen to them.

What Students Say

Research evidence shows that while what teachers believe and perceive about their practices are important, it is the students' views that count, a finding that runs counter to many current practices. In fact, educators rarely consider asking students (of any age) what they think about school and how they

---

What the Evidence Shows

Effective teachers possess a rich array of content and pedagogical knowledge but also know how to model effective teaching and learning skills; they know that who they are as individuals is as important as what they teach in influencing student learning (McCombs, 2003b, 2004a; Sato, 2000).

Effective teachers can inspire higher motivation and greater learning gains in their students—regardless of the school's poverty levels or minority status—than their less effective colleagues (McCombs & Quiat, 2002; Sanders & Rivers, 1996).

Effective teachers possess a set of characteristics related to qualities of effective helpers that include the following:

- They are highly reflective.
- They believe they can make a difference with all kinds of learners.
- They see teaching and learning as a partnership between teachers and their students.
- They believe students should have choices and be responsible for their own learning.
- They care about students and making a difference in their learning process and progress.
- They are passionate about the subject(s) they teach.
- They are experts in their fields of study. (Bransford, Brown, & Cocking, 1999; Combs, 1986; McCombs, 1999b)

Effective teachers hold core professional values that relate to the value of learning, their role as active agents in their professional world, the role of collaboration and dialogue with key partners, the value of professional dialogue with colleagues to develop collective expertise, and the value of activism and standing up for the moral purpose of teaching (Day, 2002; McCombs, 2004b).

---

would like to learn—in spite of findings from brain research that even young children have the capacity for complex thinking and that their perspectives are valid (e.g., Caine & Caine, 1997; Diamond & Hopson, 1998; Jensen, 1998; Sylwester, R., 1995; Wolfe & Sorgen, 1990).

Yet a variety of sources reveals that today's school-age children consider themselves to be living in a frightening world, have lost their sense of hope, and feel adults do not respect or listen to them. If students aren't respected and listened to, if their voices continue to be ignored, it should be no surprise

that they are increasingly alienated and disconnected from schools and from adults who ignore their perspectives. By listening to students, researchers have found more effective practices for engaging them in the process of learning.

The research also indicates the benefits of not just listening to youth, but also engaging them in authentic adult partnerships that address key issues of relevance to their lives, such as education. When asked, youth are clear about what defines schools where they love to learn. The box on the next page shows the results of Rogers and Freiberg's study

---

What Students Want From School

Students consistently reported that they want

- to be trusted and respected;
- to be part of a family;
- their teachers to act as helpers;
- opportunities to be responsible;
- freedom, not license;
- a place where people care;
- teachers who help them succeed; and
- to have choices.

SOURCE: Rogers and Freiberg (1994).

(1994) in which they asked students what motivates them to learn in school.

Glasser's (1990, 1994) Quality School model, which is consistent with the LCPs, is based on the assumption that children must make the choices and take responsibility for their own learning and performance evaluations. DuFour (1999) describes guidelines for school leaders that emphasize less control and more shared decision making among all stakeholders, including students. Kenney and Watson (1998) report that when given the chance, students contribute positively to creating new cultures of fairness and caring.

These findings show that in order to address motivation, learning, achievement, and positive functioning, it is critical that the learner be considered just as important as the learning process. This means that there must be increased attention to the personal domain, that is, the domain of educational systems design concerned with supporting the personal, motivational, learning, and interpersonal needs of all learners.

Ericson and Ellet (2002) present a powerful argument that students have incentives to undercut the intent of reforms when their views are ignored. On the other hand, researchers focused on student perspective have shown the benefits of practices that involve building learning partnerships, honoring student voices, and engaging students in personal ownership over their own learning.

For example, Mitra (2002) found that while teachers blame students for not being interested in their education or blame uninvolved parents, students point to problems such as instruction not being compatible with their learning styles and the need for additional tutoring and counseling. Such disparities in perspective suggest that a school reform model that incorporates students in the reform might focus efforts on different problems and suggest different solutions for enhancing their motivation and achievement.

Strategies for Honoring Student Voice

The power of honoring student voice is particularly clear in Mitra's (2002) research. In this research, focus groups were conducted with high school students representing a highly diverse student body, including students with a broad range of academic achievement and who belonged to a variety of social cliques. Students were asked what types of supports they needed to succeed and what was not working for them in their classes. Students were also asked to participate in the analysis of focus group data to clarify areas of needed reform.

Forming a Student Forum

The enthusiasm generated by this focus group experience caused students to organize a Student Forum that allowed them to continue to work on some of the problems they had identified. In this forum, students chose to focus on building communication and partnerships between themselves and their teachers. The Student Forum was facilitated by one of the school's teachers, but students assumed much of the responsibility for developing two complementary strategies for building communication between teachers and students:

- teacher-focused activities in which students partnered with teachers on reform work the teachers were conducting, and
- student-focused activities in which teachers partnered with students to increase their awareness of student views and needs. This helped both teachers and students to learn about each other's perspectives and to become more able to see each other's point of view.

The Student Forum members then served as "experts" in the classroom experience and provided feedback to teachers on how students might learn new pedagogical strategies and materials through participation in teacher professional development sessions. Students also made suggestions for how to make lessons more applicable to student needs and interests, and they shared insights on how students learn to read and what reading strategies would be more effective.

In their work with teachers, Student Forum members shared personal accounts in which they experienced significant learning and in which they did not learn at all. Student members also served as translators of the student and teacher experiences, including writing questions for the schoolwide writing assessment with prompts that made topics relevant and that were phrased in a language students could understand. All of these activities helped students develop confidence in their ability to share their ideas and experiences with adults.

In order for Student Forum members to serve as a bridge between student and teacher perceptions, they formed research groups to learn about curriculum, school policy, and teacher perspectives. As a result, they not only improved their own learning but also gained greater understanding of the system and felt more capable of influencing it. Students also served as an accountability mechanism in teacher meetings, which contributed to teachers behaving more professionally during these meetings.

Teacher's receptivity to the value of student opinions increased, and both teachers and students increased their ability to agree to disagree when necessary without becoming hostile. Adults who participated in the Student Forum activities also developed stronger beliefs in the value of partnering with students, and many teachers were motivated and inspired to continue to improve their practices to meet student needs.

Mitra (2002) concludes that the Student Forum experience is a promising strategy for balancing student and teacher-focused activities primarily as a result of three organizational contexts:

1. Activities are designed to influence policy and the school reform process rather than directly challenge teacher practice—a less threatening approach for teachers.

2. Students are protected from school bureaucracy by being buffered from external threats, such as policies that prohibit their involvement, which connects them to opportunities within the school by building bridges with teaching staff.

3. School reform leaders are given the authority and clout to provide information and funding, which provides inspiration, emotional support, and energy to the group.

Involving Students in Action Research Projects

In his case study of a large, comprehensive high school, Calvert (2002) studied an action research model for involving youth in school decision making through a focus on building student-teacher dialogue. This "Communities" program examined whether the action research approach could improve the school environment through fostering positive youth development and providing avenues for students to become active partners in organizational decision making. Calvert's results indicate that along with changes in the organizational culture, student-staff relations improve. Because neither students nor teachers are accustomed to such partnership roles, these changes take time to

develop, and supportive structures are needed as a way to scaffold, or support, these skills and habits.

Calvert's (2002) research revealed that before his action research project began, he found teacher and student roles to be generally structured in ways that inhibit reciprocal relationships. For instance, scheduling and time constraints often make communication between students and staff difficult, preventing students from taking significant roles in organizational decision making. As his action research project progressed, however, Calvert found that in comparison with their traditional school experiences, teachers and students became more personally satisfied with the reciprocal learning experiences resulting from the project. As a result, both staff and students came to question "traditional" structures and to examine schedules allowing more space for relationship-building.

Calvert's (2002) research supports the view that students can participate meaningfully as agents of positive change at both the classroom and school levels. For youth to be involved in meaningful decision making, Calvert argues that they must be involved in ongoing planning and implementation of both policies and programs. Students must work with adults in equitable partnerships that benefit both youth and the school community as a whole. When this partnering occurs, students bring a sense of mission that positively affects both themselves and adults.

Adults who experience collective partnering with students experience a sense of being more connected and effective in their work with their students, and they also demonstrate a change in their beliefs about both the competence and motivation of youth in general.

Students as Meaningful Partners: International Evidence

Outside the United States, particularly in Great Britain and Australia, students are being authentically included as meaningful partners in school reform. In a study of student voice in British school reform, Fielding (2000, 2001, 2002b) describes a four-year Student as Researcher project in which students identified important issues in their daily experience of schooling. Together with students, staff gathered data, constructed meaning, shared recommendations for change with fellow students and staff, and presented their recommendations to the governing body of the school.

Fielding found that students began challenging the curriculum to move it away from a delivery model to a jointly derived, negotiated curriculum and pedagogy with meaning and relevance to their own lives. As the project continued, several student-led changes emerged from the dialogue engendered by the partnership model. Students demonstrated the quality of their research and ability to identify and articulate insights into curriculum practices as they gained new understandings and insights into their learning and the nature of the learning experience. The ongoing dialogue between teachers and students showed that both groups came to view their joint efforts as reflective of a genuine community. Teachers and students developed a commitment to teaching and learning as a genuinely shared responsibility, and each redefined what it means to be a student and a teacher.

This simple idea—listening to kids in meaningful partnerships with adults as a foundation for addressing youth and public policy issues—is central to learner-centered teaching, to empowering youth, and to changing many systemic inequities and failures. Meaningful change and positive growth have consistently been found to derive from supportive and caring relationships between and among youth and adults (e.g., Lambert & McCombs, 1998; McCombs & Whisler, 1997; Rudduck, Day, & Wallace, 1997). Cook-Sather (2002) has argued that in such contexts, students not only have the knowledge and position to shape what counts in education, but they can help change power dynamics and create new forums for learning how to speak out for themselves.

A focus on schools as systems can change the status quo and gain institutional support for more transformative views. As a result, the necessary conditions for improving student achievement and motivation for learning are created. Fielding supports constructing practices and programs for teachers and students to "make meaning" together in learning communities "in which the voices of students, teachers and others are acknowledged as legitimately different and of equal value, the necessary partners in dialogue about how we learn, how we live, and the kind of place we wish our community to become" (Fielding, 2002a, p. 13).

> It's not that I wasn't good before . . . but I'm better. I'm much better. And more students leave my room thinking that I *did* have an impact on their learning. (A ninth-grade English teacher in a learner-centered suburban high school)
> Personally, for me, it was a career saver. I moved away from delivering the same old curriculum in the same way year after year

> to a new and different approach to dealing with human beings—kids in my classroom. It's rejuvenated my career. (Another teacher from a rural high school)

As a way to get to know your students a bit better, have them complete the "Getting to Know You" sheet on the next page. Record in your journal what you observed during this activity.

Reflection

Whew! What does all this mean for you and your teaching? To begin thinking about it, take a moment to reflect on your own experiences on your journey with students. Take a deep breath, close your eyes, and ask yourself the following questions:

- Do I **know** how my students perceive my teaching practices?
- Do I really **believe** that all students are capable learners?
- What do I **want to do** to reach those students who seem "difficult" to me?
- What are my **fears** about developing learning partnerships with my students?

What's Next?

Now that you have a better idea of what the research shows regarding what "learner-centered" means, how being learner-centered fits into the bigger picture of education as a living system, the growing support for learner-centered principles and practices, and what lies at the heart of these practices, you're ready to take a deeper look at the Learner-Centered Principles, the topic of Chapter 4. The pace of the journey slows a bit as we delve into the LCPs one by one, along with their implications for practice.

Getting to Know You Sheet and Creative Name Tag

GETTING TO KNOW YOU

Please fill in the following information about yourself. Turn this in to your teacher so that she or he can learn more about you.

1. My nickname is _____.

2. I have _____ (how many) brothers and sisters.

3. My favorite thing to do at school is _____.

4. My favorite school subject is _____.

5. My favorite book is _____.

6. If I could learn about anything, I would like to learn _____

   _____.

7. A good teacher is one who _____.

8. I think school should help me to _____.

9. I learn best when I _____.

10. Activities that do not help me learn are _____

    _____.

11. When I grow up, I want to be _____.

12. If I were going to describe the kind of person I am, I would say _____

    _____

    _____.

Directions: Fill this in for yourself. Find someone you don't know. Share your Creative Name Tags with each other. Without interrupting each other, take turns telling each other what you think the other person's name tag says about him or her. When both are done, you can talk and correct each other if necessary.

Creative Name Tag

Draw what you do well.

Draw what you like to do.

Draw a value.

List 4 words that are you.

SOURCE: Dr. H. Jerome Freiberg, University of Houston, Consistency Management and Cooperative Discipline Department (1995). Used with permission.

4

The Learner-Centered Principles

One by One

By now you have developed a good understanding of what learner centered is—and probably what it isn't. In addition, you also have a good idea of the research underlying the validity of the Learner-Centered Model (LCM). To help you understand the LCM more thoroughly, we now invite you to the next stop on your journey: an opportunity for you to develop your understanding of each of the 14 Learner-Centered Psychological Principles (LCPs) that have been adopted by the American Psychological Association (APA). As you recall from our discussion in Chapter 2 (as shown in Figure 2.4), these principles are categorized into four major domains, or factors, that affect learners and learning. These domains refer to major areas of human functioning that are holistically involved in the process of learning—for all learners, cradle to grave:

- Cognitive and metacognitive—the intellectual capacities of learners and how they facilitate the learning process.
- Motivational and affective—the roles played by motivation and emotions in learning.
- Developmental and social—the influence of various diverse aspects of learner development and the importance of interpersonal interactions in learning and change.
- Individual differences—how individual differences influence learning; how teachers, students, and administrators adapt to learning diversity; and how standards and assessment can best support individual differences in learners.

Although all 14 principles and all four domains define those factors involved in learning for each individual learner, looking at each domain and principle in more detail affords you the opportunity to construct your own meaning and understanding, which then allows you to understand

Figure 4.1   Domains/Factors Influencing Learners and Learning and Associated Learner-Centered Principles (LCPs)

Domain	Associated Learner-Centered Principles (LCPs)
Cognitive and Metacognitive Factors	1. Nature of the learning process 2. Goals of the learning process 3. Construction of knowledge 4. Strategic thinking 5. Thinking about thinking 6. Context of learning
Motivational and Affective Factors	7. Motivational and emotional influences on learning 8. Intrinsic motivation to learn 9. Effects of motivation on effort
Developmental and Social Factors	10. Developmental influences on learning 11. Social influences on learning
Individual Differences Factors	12. Individual differences in learning 13. Learning and diversity 14. Standards and assessment

the meaning of these principles and their implications for practice at the classroom and school levels.

In each of the following four sections, we describe the domains affecting learners and learning and the LCPs associated with each domain. The schematic in Figure 4.1 shows the organizational scheme of these four sections.

Domain 1: Cognitive and Metacognitive Factors

When most people think of learning, they think about the intellectual or brain functions (cognitive and metacognitive) that are involved. The cognitive and metacognitive factors involved in learning have been studied extensively over the past century, helping us to understand more clearly what cognitive and metacognitive learning are and how we best learn using these brain processes and capacities. These terms, "cognitive" and "metacognitive," have come to be understood in specific ways.

Cognition generally includes memorization of information or content or other processes and strategies we use to acquire, process, retrieve, and store information (Bransford, Brown, & Cocking, 1999; Gay, 2001; Livingston,

1997; Zimmerman & Schunk, 2001). More specifically, "cognitive" is generally defined as those learning processes that have to do with information storage, retrieval, processing, and acquisition or reception. Cognitive learning involves various brain functions and capabilities generally associated with the thinking, reasoning, and perceiving aspects of learning new information.

Metacognition generally refers to "thinking about thinking." These higher-order processes involved in overseeing one's thinking or cognitive processes are said to include an executive level of awareness for monitoring and regulating thinking and learning processes and strategies (Hacker, Dunlosky, & Graesser, 1998; Lambert & McCombs, 1998; McCombs, 2001; McCombs & Whisler, 1997; Zimmerman & Schunk, 2001). There is also a knowledge component in which humans know about their own learning processes (Livingston, 1997).

With this general background, then, let's delve into the LCPs, one by one, associated with the four cognitive and metacognitive domains under which they fall. As we introduce each principle, we have put the text from the original LCPs document (APA, 1997) in italics.

LCP 1: Nature of the Learning Process

The learning of complex subject matter is most effective when it is an intentional process of constructing meaning from information and experience.

There are different types of learning processes, for example, habit formation in motor learning and learning that involves the generation of knowledge, or cognitive skills and learning strategies. Learning in schools emphasizes students' use of intentional processes to construct meaning from information, experiences, and their own thoughts and beliefs. Successful learners are active, goal-directed, self-regulating, and assume personal responsibility for contributing to their own learning. The principles set forth in this document focus on this type of learning.

Parents and teachers of young children can clearly see that they want and yearn to learn and know about their world. As children get older, they want to know about values and how life works so they can make wise decisions. Developmental psychologists and brain researchers have discovered that even very young children are capable of learning strategies for more efficiently and effectively processing and remembering new information (Bransford et al., 1999). Just listening to young children learn their "ABC's" with the Alphabet Song is proof of this! Test your understanding using Activity LCP 1.

LCP 2: Goals of the Learning Process

The successful learner, over time and with support and instructional guidance, can create meaningful, coherent representations of knowledge.

The strategic nature of learning requires students to be goal directed. To construct useful representations of knowledge and to acquire the thinking and learning strategies necessary for continued learning success across their life span, students must generate and pursue personally relevant goals. Initially, students' short-term goals and learning may be sketchy in an area, but over time their understanding can be refined by filling gaps, resolving inconsistencies, and

ACTIVITY LCP 1

Test Your Understanding of LCP 1: Nature of the Learning Process

Create a mnemonic to help students learn some factual information about something of interest to them. Then create a mnemonic to help them learn something you think they should know but are not going to test, whether or not they are interested. Compare their recall of the two mnemonic devices after several days have passed.

First mnemonic:

Second mnemonic:

Students' recall using mnemonic 1:

Students' recall using mnemonic 2:

Your observations about any differences between their recall using the two mnemonics:

---

deepening their understanding of the subject matter so that they can reach longer-term goals. Educators can assist learners in creating meaningful learning goals that are consistent with both personal and educational aspirations and interests.

Whether we know it or not, most of what we learn is directed at some personal goal. What most of us recognize in our work with students in classrooms is that it is difficult for many students to have goals related to much of what they are required to learn. Much of the information seems irrelevant and boring to students. If we can understand the role goals play in energizing and shaping the learning process, we can more readily help students think about short- and long-term goals and how learning new information can fit into these goals (Lambert & McCombs, 1998; McCombs & Whisler, 1997). Test your understanding using Activity LCP 2.

ACTIVITY LCP 2

Test Your Understanding of LCP 2: Goals of the Learning Process

Create a goal-setting exercise to help students see the relevance of some factual information. During the exercise, help the students construct the relationship between what they want to know (learn, do, be) and the factual information at hand. For instance, if they are interested in hip hop (rap), help them construct the relationship between hip hop and poetry: the rhythm of rhyming, alliterations, metaphors, and thematic elements—all aspects of English literacy that become relevant when seen from the perspective of rapping. Record any observations you have here.

LCP 3: Construction of Knowledge

The successful learner can link new information with existing knowledge in meaningful ways.

Knowledge widens and deepens as students continue to build links between new information and experiences and their existing knowledge base. The nature of these links can take a variety of forms, such as adding to, modifying, or reorganizing existing knowledge or skills. How these links are made or develop may vary in different subject areas, and among students with varying talents, interests, and abilities. However, unless new knowledge becomes integrated with the learner's prior knowledge and understanding, this new knowledge remains isolated, cannot be used most effectively in new tasks, and does not transfer readily to new situations. Educators can assist learners in acquiring and integrating knowledge by a number of strategies that have been shown to *be effective with learners of varying abilities, such as concept mapping and thematic organization or categorizing.*

Students of all ages want to make sense of the world (Bransford et al., 1999). We all learn to make sense of new information by linking it to information we already know. To make this link, most of us find it most helpful to have examples of how the new information links to prior experiences. We teachers can play a vital role in helping students to verbalize what new information means to them and how it might be related to their talents, interests, or abilities. We can teach students strategies for organizing and categorizing information in ways that make sense to them. When students share their strategies with their teachers and classmates, each learner has the opportunity to get feedback and refine his or her understanding. Test your understanding using Activity LCP 3.

ACTIVITY LCP 3

Test Your Understanding of LCP 3: Construction of Knowledge

Create a strategy to help students relate and organize new factual information to information they may already know. For instance, using the poetry–hip hop illustration from the previous activity (LCP 2), you might have your students each draw a web diagram that shows what they already know about poetry from their knowledge of hip hop. Have them include blank spaces for the new factual information they discover about the elements poetry and hip hop share: rhyming, the rhythm of rhyme, alliterations, assonance, imagery, personification, metaphors, onomatopoeia, point of view, repetition, stanza, and thematic elements (feel free to add more!). Describe your strategy and any observations you have about what happened here.

LCP 4: Strategic Thinking

The successful learner can create and use a repertoire of thinking and reasoning strategies to achieve complex learning goals.

Successful learners use strategic thinking in their approach to learning, reasoning, problem solving, and concept learning. They understand and can use a variety of strategies to help them reach learning and performance goals and to apply their knowledge in novel situations. They also continue to expand their repertoire of strategies by reflecting on the methods they use to see which work well for them, by receiving guided instruction and feedback, and by observing or interacting with appropriate models. Learning outcomes can be enhanced if educators assist learners in developing, applying, and assessing their strategic learning skills.

One of life's best teachers is a model. In fact, we learn about 80% of what we know from watching others—our parents, our teachers, our heroes, the media, and so on (McCombs & Whisler, 1997). When we model effective strategies for learning new information or for solving learning problems, our students are more likely to use them as well. Students can also benefit from explicit instruction in various kinds of learning strategies, such as those for comprehending what they are reading, finding their logic errors in math problems, or solving a mathematical word problem. Test your understanding using Activity LCP 4.

ACTIVITY LCP 4

Test Your Understanding of LCP 4: Strategic Thinking

Create a modeling technique you could use to help students learn some factual information from a course you teach. For instance, you might create a spreadsheet that shows individual poems and hip hop songs down the page, and types of poetic devices across the page: rhyming, the rhythm of rhyme, alliterations, assonance, imagery, personification, metaphors, onomatopoeia, point of view, repetition, stanza, and thematic elements (feel free to add more!). You can show your students how, for each poem you read and hip hop song you hear/read, you can indicate the devices used and list examples. Then you can demonstrate how you might use the spreadsheet to discover which devices are most common, which have the greatest impact on you and why, and which you want to use in a poem or song. Record your technique here.

LCP 5: Thinking About Thinking

Higher-order strategies for selecting and monitoring mental operations facilitate creative and critical thinking.

Successful learners can reflect on how they think and learn, set reasonable learning or performance goals, select potentially appropriate learning strategies or methods, and monitor their progress toward those goals. In addition, successful learners know what to do if a problem occurs or if they are not making sufficient or timely progress toward a goal. They can generate alternative methods to reach their goal (or reassess the appropriateness and utility of the goal). Instructional methods that focus on helping learners develop these higher-order (metacognitive) strategies can enhance student learning and personal responsibility for learning.

For students to learn higher-order or metacognitive strategies for monitoring and regulating their own learning, they need time to reflect on what they are learning, how they are learning it, the progress they are making, and any problems or concerns they may have while learning (Lambert & McCombs, 1998; McCombs, 2001). Under pressure to cover curriculum and prepare students for assessments, we frequently fail to give them a chance to engage in the reflection and self-inquiry that underlie metacognition. Because these processes facilitate the development of metacognitive skills and strategies, we greatly increase our students' probability of becoming responsible, lifelong learners when we create opportunities for them to explore and develop these metacognitive skills. Test your understanding using Activity LCP 5.

ACTIVITY LCP 5

Test Your Understanding of LCP 5: Thinking About Thinking

Create a reflection or self-inquiry exercise to help students plan the process they will follow in writing a poem or song. For instance, have your students use a list of questions as they plan their writing:

- What do I already know about poetic devices?

- What experience do I have with poetic devices? Which poetic devices do I have most experience with?

- Which poetic devices will I use in this poem/song?

- How will each poetic device help my listeners/readers understand what I'm trying to communicate?

- What do I want my classmates to take away from listening to my poem/song? Record your reflections and thoughts here.

LCP 6: Context of Learning

Learning is influenced by environmental factors, including culture, technology, and instructional practices.

Learning does not occur in a vacuum. Teachers play a major interactive role with both the learner and the learning environment. Cultural or group influences on students can impact many educationally relevant variables, such as motivation, orientation toward learning, and ways of thinking. Technologies and instructional practices must be appropriate for learners' level of prior knowledge, cognitive abilities, and their learning and thinking strategies. The classroom environment, particularly the degree to which it is nurturing or not, can also have significant impact on student learning.

All students are influenced by the social and physical context of the classroom. How technology is used, whether students can work in pairs or with other students, how diverse student learning needs are handled by the teacher, and a variety of other contextual factors influence how students view the learning process in general and their own learning abilities in particular (Bransford et al., 1999; Lambert & McCombs, 1998; McCombs & Vakili, 2005). The teacher plays a major role in establishing a positive learning context in which all learners feel valued and capable of learning. Test your understanding using Activity LCP 6.

ACTIVITY LCP 6

Test Your Understanding of LCP 6: Context of Learning

List the strategies you use to establish a positive classroom context that helps your students learn. For instance, what do you do to establish your classroom as a community within which learning is expected to occur; to incorporate technology in the most efficient and effective ways for your particular students' needs; and to tailor and fine tune your instructional strategies so they meet your individual students' needs?

Domain 2: Motivational and Affective Factors

LCP 7: Motivational and Emotional Influences on Learning

What and how much is learned is influenced by the learner's motivation. Motivation to learn, in turn, is influenced by the individual's emotional state, beliefs, interests and goals, and habits of thinking.

The rich internal world of thoughts, beliefs, goals, and expectations for success or failure can enhance or interfere with the learner's quality of thinking and information processing. Students' beliefs about themselves as learners and the nature of learning have a marked influence on motivation. Motivational and emotional factors also influence both the quality of thinking and information processing as well as an individual's motivation to learn. Positive emotions, such as curiosity, generally enhance motivation and facilitate learning and performance. Mild anxiety can also enhance learning and performance by *focusing the learner's attention on a particular task. However, intense negative emotions (e.g., anxiety, panic, rage, insecurity) and related thoughts (e.g., worrying about competence; ruminating about failure; fearing punishment, ridicule, or stigmatizing labels) generally detract from motivation, interfere with learning, and contribute to low performance.*

Motivation to learn is natural in young children—as evidenced by their insatiable curiosity to explore, discover, and know. For many of us, however, that natural motivation can become hidden or lost in some learning situations. Apparent lack of motivation is largely due to negative thoughts we have about ourselves and our abilities, or even about the learning situation, including our teacher. If learners of any age are worried about their chances of success or how they will be viewed by others, just two of a host of possibilities, they often experience fear and anxiety, which then override their positive emotions of curiosity and interest. When fear and/or anxiety take over, information processing and other cognitive functions are impaired, and performance suffers (McCombs & Whisler, 1997). When teachers are aware of the debilitating effects of negative self-thoughts, they can assist students by providing a variety of supports and success experiences that build confidence and motivation. Test your understanding using Activity LCP 7.

ACTIVITY LCP 7

Test Your Understanding of LCP 7:
Motivational and Emotional Influences on Learning

Create a list of strategies you use to help students who demonstrate low motivation to learn and/or fear or anxiety about learning a subject. For instance, consider how your students respond when you tailor and fine tune your instructional strategies to meet their individual learning needs. Which strategies seem to work best for students who learn primarily through visual-spatial processes? Through linguistic processes? Through physical processes? Through logical and/or mathematical processes? Through working alone? Through working in teams or groups?

LCP 8: Intrinsic Motivation to Learn

The learner's creativity, higher-order thinking, and natural curiosity all contribute to motivation to learn. Intrinsic motivation is stimulated by tasks of optimal novelty and difficulty, relevant to personal interests and providing for personal choice and control.

Curiosity, flexible and insightful thinking, and creativity are major indicators of the learners' intrinsic motivation to learn, which is, in large part, a function of meeting basic needs to be competent and to exercise personal control. Intrinsic motivation is facilitated on tasks that learners perceive as interesting and personally relevant and meaningful, appropriate in complexity and difficulty to the learners' abilities, and on which they believe they can succeed. Intrinsic motivation is also facilitated on tasks that are comparable to real-world situations and meet needs for choice and control. Educators can encourage and support learners' natural curiosity and motivation to learn by attending to individual differences in learners' perceptions of optimal novelty and difficulty, relevance, and personal choice and control.

In a typical school, students are often asked to learn things that they are not naturally interested in or curious about learning. It then becomes the teacher's job to figure out how to make what students have to learn more meaningful, interesting, and relevant to their interests and experiences. Those who have studied what triggers natural or intrinsic motivation to learn have found that there are three major conditions or needs that must be satisfied in school in order for intrinsic motivation to learn to surface. Teachers must help students feel

- competent and able to succeed,
- autonomous and self-determining,
- like they belong and fit in. (Deci & Ryan, 1985, 1990)

Rather than blaming students for what looks like lack of motivation, teachers who understand this principle know that they just need to alter the conditions and context of learning by helping all students experience success and feelings of competence, by allowing developmentally appropriate choices of learning experiences, and by creating learning communities and positive relationships in which all students feel like they belong. If we want students to become self-directed and self-regulated learners, it is particularly critical that they have opportunities for choice and control—without which they will merely become compliant learners, or they will choose to disrupt and/or leave school (McCombs, 2001, 2004b). Test your understanding using Activity LCP 8.

ACTIVITY LCP 8

Test Your Understanding of LCP 8: Intrinsic Motivation to Learn

Create a list of strategies you use to meet students' basic needs for competence, autonomy, and belonging. For instance, what do you do to set up your classroom as a community within which your students feel they are valued members? How do you make certain each student is challenged just enough to have to "stretch," yet not enough to feel as if s/he is failing or incompetent? What do you do to make certain your students have opportunities to choose what they will learn and how? Describe your strategies here.

LCP 9: Effects of Motivation on Effort

Acquisition of complex knowledge and skills requires extended learner effort and guided practice. Without learners' motivation to learn, the willingness to exert this effort is unlikely without coercion.

Effort is another major indicator of motivation to learn. The acquisition of complex knowledge and skills demands the investment of considerable learner energy and strategic effort, along with persistence over time. Educators need to be concerned with facilitating motivation by strategies that enhance learner effort and commitment to learning and to achieving high standards of comprehension and understanding. Effective strategies include purposeful *learning activities, guided by practices that enhance positive emotions and intrinsic motivation to learn, and methods that increase learners' perceptions that a task is interesting and personally relevant.*

When students are free of negative thoughts or fears that interfere with their natural curiosity and motivation to learn—and when they are supported in basic needs that give rise to their intrinsic motivation to learn—they freely put effort into learning. Evidence of this effort is that students use active learning strategies such as paying attention to things the teacher says, doing the assignments or even going beyond what is asked, persisting when learning gets difficult, and challenging themselves to do even harder work

(Meece, Herman, & McCombs, 2003). When learners are being effortful and strategic during learning, they are engaged and learning to optimal levels. Teachers can facilitate student effort and commitment to learning by involving their students as active partners in decisions about learning experiences that are of most interest and relevance to them, and by meeting student needs to be successful and to belong. Peer learning and inquiry-based learning are examples of practices that provide students with opportunities to put forth considerable effort to learn information, skills, and processes they are motivated to learn. In peer learning, students take turns being the teacher and learner—cementing their knowledge by learning it more deeply. In inquiry-based learning, students pose their own questions that are of highest interest to them in a given content area—letting interest be the engine that deepens their learning. Test your understanding using Activity LCP 9.

ACTIVITY LCP 9

Test Your Understanding of LCP 9: Effects of Motivation on Effort

Create a list of strategies you use to promote student effort and strategic learning. For instance, peer learning and inquiry-based learning are two strategies that promote student effort and strategic learning. Another is project-based learning. List others you have used with your students. Describe in your journal what you have observed about your students' increased motivation and their improved strategic learning that resulted from their learning through any of these practices. Did you observe that some practices increased motivation more than others? Did some practices result in more improved strategic thinking than others? If so, how would you explain the differences? Describe your strategies here.

Domain 3: Developmental and Social Factors

One of the areas that has been most researched and has produced the strongest evidence supporting learner-centered practices has to do with the types of developmental changes in learners over time and the critical role of supportive adult-student relationships in both development and learning (McCombs, 2004a; McCombs & Whisler, 1997). To truly make a difference in the lives and achievement of our students, we need a deep understanding of how developmental and social factors influence their (and our) learning.

It has long been recognized that humans have a need and tendency to form social connections. We also share many qualities—such as empathy, kindness, compassion, love, friendship, and hope—that represent our spirituality. These spiritual qualities are based on social relationships, which is where these qualities are developed and from which they emerge. Making meaning or sense out of life by creating organizational structures is also central to how we become social and spiritual.

A useful metaphor for understanding the developmental differences that emerge in classrooms and schools is to see schools as organizational structures consisting of an interlocking series of social relationships that directly impact students' (and teachers') lives. In contrast to mechanical or solitary computer metaphors that do not do justice to the interconnectivity of humans (Cacioppo, Hawkley, Rickett, & Masi, 2005), this social relationship metaphor of school allows us to see that understanding the social qualities underlying teaching and learning can lead to respect for the developmental differences that emerge in classrooms and schools.

LCP 10: Developmental Influence on Learning

As individuals develop, there are different opportunities and constraints for learning. Learning is most effective when differential development within and across physical, intellectual, emotional, and social domains is taken into account.

Individuals learn best when material is appropriate to their developmental level and is presented in an enjoyable and interesting way. Because individual development varies across intellectual, social, emotional, and physical domains, achievement in different instructional domains may also vary. Overemphasis on one type of developmental readiness—such as reading readiness, for example—may preclude learners from demonstrating that they are more capable in other areas of performance. The cognitive, emotional, and social development of individual learners and how they interpret life experiences are affected by prior schooling, home, culture, and community factors.

Early and continuing parental involvement in schooling, and the quality of language interactions and two-way communications between adults and children, can influence these developmental areas. Awareness and understanding of developmental differences among children with and without emotional, physical, or intellectual disabilities can facilitate the creation of optimal learning contexts.

The thought of having to be aware of and know the developmental differences in your students in order to create the "right" instructional and contextual experiences for individual learning can be daunting! However, the key to meeting the diverse student needs represented by your students is to combine your knowledge of individual students with the basic principles of human development. A good place to begin is with two excellent books on child and adolescent development, one by Meece (2002) and one by Fabes and Martin (2003). Meece's book, written especially for educators, focuses on the development of school-age and adolescent students. She addresses various aspects of development, including cognition; social, emotional, and moral development; language and literacy; individual differences in development; and children with special needs. Fabes and Martin describe the social, biological, and cultural factors that influence child and adolescent development. Specifically, they discuss the dynamic interplay among physical, psychological, and cultural differences; gender; race; ethnicity; and social and economic status.

You are probably already attending to individual differences among your students. For example, listening to students; creating caring learning communities in the classroom; and implementing peer tutoring, learning strategies, teacher teaming, and looping strategies are some effective ways to deal with developmental differences without feeling overwhelmed. All of these strategies involve students in learning with and from each other, involve you in working with and learning from your colleagues, or allow you to stay with the same students for multiple years and thus more deeply build the relationships essential to adapting to individual differences. Test your understanding using Activity LCP 10.

ACTIVITY LCP 10

Test Your Understanding of LCP 10: Developmental Influences on Learning

List the strategies you use to meet your students' developmental differences in each of the following areas:

- emotional,
- physical,
- visual-spatial,
- quantitative/mathematical,
- musical,
- linguistic,
- intellectual,
- social.

For instance, if you use projects in your teaching, how do you help students select and design projects that account for their individual developmental needs in each of the areas in the preceding list? If you use team teaching, how do you and your colleagues design instruction to meet individual developmental needs? How do you assist your students in learning about their own developmental profile across the areas in the preceding list? List your strategies here.

LCP 11: Social Influences on Learning

Learning is influenced by social interactions, interpersonal relations, and communication with others.

Learning can be enhanced when the learner has an opportunity to interact and to collaborate with others on instructional tasks. Learning settings that allow for social interactions, and that respect diversity, encourage flexible thinking and social competence. In interactive and collaborative instructional contexts, individuals have an opportunity for perspective taking and reflective thinking that may lead to higher levels of cognitive, social, and moral development, as well as self-esteem. Quality personal relationships that provide stability, trust, and caring can increase learners' sense of belonging, self-respect, and self-acceptance, and provide a positive climate for learning. Family influences, positive interpersonal support, and instruction in self-motivation strategies can offset factors that interfere with optimal learning such as negative beliefs about competence in a particular subject, high levels of test anxiety, negative sex role expectations, and undue pressure to perform well. Positive learning climates can also help to establish the context for healthier levels of thinking, feeling, and behaving. Such contexts help learners feel safe to share ideas, actively participate in the learning process, and create a learning community.

Decades of research have confirmed the importance of student-teacher relationships in student motivation, social outcomes, and classroom learning. Further benefits of having a good relationship with teachers are that students experience their academic work as meaningful, personal, complementing their other goals, and promoting their understanding. By contrast, when students experience poor relationships with their teachers, they see their academic work as coercive, repetitive, isolated, irrelevant, and contrary to their social and academic goals. Good relationships are defined by low levels of conflict and high levels of closeness and support. Through these relationships, children learn how to regulate their behavior and affect and develop social competence (Davis, 2006).

Research has also shown that not only is learning facilitated in positive social contexts, but the quality of thinking, creativity, and problem solving also improves (Rudduck, Day, & Wallace, 1997). Caring classroom and school environments have also been shown to significantly influence positive development of the whole learner as well as lead to higher levels of achievement in reading and math (Noddings, 2005). More specifically, Noddings has shown that the ingredients necessary for students to develop strong relationships with

teachers who care about them include opportunities to

- build community and mutual respect,
- create social responsibility,
- develop an appreciation for diversity,
- develop emotional literacy, and
- manage and resolve conflict.

In our own research, we have shown with over 30,000 students from kindergarten through college that the most important predictor of student motivation and a range of positive academic and nonacademic outcomes is students' perceptions that their teachers create positive relationships and a positive climate for learning (McCombs, 2004b; Meece et al., 2003; Perry & Daniels, 2004; Pierce, Holt, Kolar, & McCombs, 2004). When teachers create learning communities that foster positive student-teacher relationships and positive student-student relationships, the most important aspect of teaching has been established. These learning communities can then function as the partnership in which students share responsibility for their learning. Test your understanding using Activity LCP 11.

Domain 4: Individual Differences Factors

When educators hear the term "learner centered," they often assume that they must do something totally different and individualized to meet the needs of each of their learners. Not only is this an overwhelming prospect, but it turns out that this is not what the evidence regarding learner-centered instruction shows. We have learned in our research that if teachers start with building positive relationships, a positive climate for

ACTIVITY LCP 11

Test Your Understanding of LCP 11: Social Influences on Learning

List the strategies you use to meet your students' developmental differences in each of the following areas:

- a sense of community and mutual respect for others;
- social responsibility within the classroom, school, and larger community;
- appreciation for various types of diversity within the classroom, school, and larger community;
- emotional literacy, or the ability to recognize, understand, process, and appropriately express emotions;
- managing and resolving conflict within the classroom, school, and larger community.

Don't worry if you have only one or a few strategies to list; as you continue your reading and learning, you can add to your list. List your strategies here.

_____

_____

_____

_____

_____

_____

learning, and caring learning communities, they are halfway finished with the "job" of individualizing (McCombs, 2004a). However, it is important for us to understand the role that individual differences play in the learning process and the implications of diversity, especially in the process of designing high standards for learning and fashioning assessment strategies that maximize learning for all students.

LCP 12: Individual Differences in Learning

Learners have different strategies, approaches, and capabilities for learning that are a function of prior experience and heredity.

Individuals are born with and develop their own capabilities and talents. In addition, through learning and social acculturation, they have acquired their own preferences for how they like to learn and the pace at which they learn. However, these preferences are not always useful in helping learners reach their learning goals. Educators need to help students examine their learning preferences and expand or modify them, if necessary. The interaction between learner differences and curricular and environmental conditions is another key factor affecting learning outcomes. Educators need to be sensitive to individual differences, in general. They also need to attend to learner perceptions of the degree to which these differences are accepted and *adapted to by varying instructional methods and materials.*

We all know that no two learners learn in the same way. Each of us has preferences for how we learn, and over the years of educational experiences we have also learned what kind of approaches usually work best for us. Each of us has at least some idea about our interests, talents, and special capabilities. As we saw earlier, these are often keys to motivating students if we teachers know our students individually and personally.

A recent report of a special National Study Group for the Affirmative Development of Academic Ability (2004) is a helpful reference. It crafted a vision for affirming academic ability, nurturing intellective competence, and moving all students to high levels of academic achievement. A particular focus was minority and low-income students and the development of competencies that could eliminate the academic achievement gaps among various groups of children. Specific competencies that were addressed included literacy and numeracy, mathematical and verbal reasoning, problem solving, sensitivity to multiple contexts and perspectives, relationship skills, self-regulation, resource recognition and help-seeking, and skill in accessing and managing information. The study group contended that "affirmative development of academic ability is nurtured and developed through (1) high-quality

---

ACTIVITY LCP 12

Test Your Understanding of LCP 12: Individual Differences in Learning

List the strategies you use to address the individual differences of the students in your classroom. If you are just beginning this process, you will be interested in Howard Gardner's concept of Multiple Intelligences (MI), which illustrates that each person is naturally attracted to certain ways of learning and thinking (Gardner, 1999). Through learning about MI, students (and their teachers!) discover how they are smart, how they naturally attend, learn, and think, and how they are each unique in their specific patterns of being smart. Describe how you could use MI to learn about your students' individual differences and teach them about their unique learning processes at the same time.

---

teaching and instruction in the classroom, (2) trusting relationships in school, and (3) supports for pro-academic behavior in the school and community" (p. 1). Test your understanding using Activity LCP 12.

LCP 13: Learning and Diversity

Learning is most effective when differences in learners' linguistic, cultural, and social backgrounds are taken into account.

The same basic principles of learning, motivation, and effective instruction apply to all learners. However, language, ethnicity, race, beliefs, and socioeconomic status all can influence learning. Careful attention to these factors in the instructional setting enhances the possibilities for designing and implementing appropriate learning environments. When learners perceive that their individual differences in abilities, backgrounds, cultures, and experiences are valued, respected, and accommodated in learning tasks and contexts, levels of motivation and achievement are enhanced.

In spite of the busy and complex life of the classrooms, learner-centered teachers understand how important it is to get to know each student personally. Every interaction with students at risk of academic failure is an opportunity to get to know individual students, their talents, and their interests. Many children with difficult backgrounds become passive and withdrawn because they don't believe teachers are going to allow them to use their strengths (Collins, 2005). To counter this belief, learner-centered teachers make sure their students are provided with equal opportunity to learn, which requires not treating them the same. This means that students from different ethnic, cultural, and socioeconomic groups may need different types of supports to enhance their learning (Rodriguez, 2005). If you adhere to the foundational principle of learner-centered practice, you will know what type of supports your students need. In other words, you will learn what your students need if you know them individually and if you establish a positive relationship with each student. The strategies for

ACTIVITY LCP 13

Test Your Understanding of LCP 13: Learning and Diversity

Create a list of strategies you use to address student diversity in a course you teach. If you are new to addressing student diversity, one simple approach is to have students report to their peers about the family traditions in their families, which they learn about through interviews with one or more family "elders." In addition, children's and adolescent literature offers a rich source of material for learning about and discussing diversity. A third approach is to have your students analyze the diversity they see on television according to categories such as:

- socio-economic status (SES), also referred to as class;
- race;
- gender;
- age;
- religion;
- sexual orientation;
- physical/mental disabilities;
- nationalities;
- political beliefs; and
- others students identify.

Describe how you could use family traditions, literature, and/or popular media to increase your students' (and your) understanding of diversity.

accomplishing this foundational domain of practice are easier than you may imagine. We discuss them in depth in Chapter 6. Test your understanding using Activity LCP 13.

LCP 14: Standards and Assessment

Setting appropriately high and challenging standards and assessing the learner as well as learning progress—including diagnostic, process, and outcome assessment—are integral parts of the learning process.

Assessment provides important information to both the learner and teacher at all stages of the learning process. Effective learning takes place when learners feel challenged to work toward appropriately high goals; therefore, appraisal of the learner's cognitive strengths and weaknesses, as well as current knowledge and skills, is important for the selection of instructional materials of an optimal degree of difficulty. Ongoing assessment of the learner's understanding of the curricular material can provide valuable feedback to both learners and teachers about progress toward the learning goals. Standardized assessment of learner progress and outcomes provides one type of information about achievement levels both within and across individuals that can inform various types of programmatic decisions. Performance assessments can provide other sources of information about the attainment of learning outcomes. Self-assessments of learning progress can also improve students' self-appraisal skills and enhance motivation and self-directed learning.

Rigorous, standards-based curriculum *and* strong social support systems that include people who value students and their learning are both successful practices that reduce the achievement gap (Gordon, 2004). For success in urban schools, in particular, promoting a positive culture is essential, including caring connections, positive behavioral supports, and teaching social and emotional skills (Osher & Fleischman, 2005).

In environments where the focus is on student performance on high-stakes tests, teachers are less inclined to encourage students to explore concepts and subjects of interest to them—obstructing students' path to becoming lifelong, self-directed learners. High-stakes testing does not adequately deal with issues in the education of low-income and non-English-speaking students and can lead to teaching to the test and inflated and/or misleading test scores. In fact, in recent years several schools and districts have experienced instances in which their test scores have been challenged either because entire groups of student scores have disappeared or were simply not included in the data collection process, or because students and/or teachers changed answers on the tests in order to skew the data in their favor (National Public Radio, 2005).

Effective approaches include engaging students in self-evaluation and meaningful feedback through formative assessment, which particularly benefits students who are achieving below their peers. Incentives are needed for low-achieving students to be motivated to work hard on high-stakes tests, such as feedback on their progress, tangible rewards, and support from their teachers to find meaning in the experience and take responsibility for their learning. A simplistic policy to use high-stakes tests will not work by itself without these extra learner-centered supports.

Schools with large numbers of students from families living in poverty are under increased pressure to spend the majority of class time on test preparation; this does not engage them in the types of strategies that will pay off in the long run (Moon, Callahan, & Tomlinson, 2003). More curriculum depth and uncrowding the curriculum will benefit teachers more, allowing them to find time to teach their students how to deal with a changing world. In addition to knowing how the world works, students need to know who they are as learners and how to go about learning what they will need in order to participate in the larger community outside school.

Learner-centered practices are part of an international movement to bring a time-honored and evidence-based set of values to education (Russell, 2004). The Learner-Centered Model is one that parents favor, according to Diamond (2005), because it would allow their children to see their learning improvement, develop necessary skills, and be prepared for higher education as well as the workplace. Test your understanding using Activity LCP 14.

ACTIVITY LCP 14

Test Your Understanding of LCP 14: Standards and Assessment

List the standards of achievement and performance you and your students have determined to be important for their learning and development. How do you and your students assess their performance and achievement? If your school, district, and/or state require the administration of high-stakes tests, describe how you offer students opportunities to set their own goals for learning and assess their progress toward those goals.

Finding Examples of LCPs in Your Own Practices

Now that you have had an opportunity to reflect more deeply on all 14 LCPs, it is time in your journey to take a look at what meaning you construct for each of these principles in your own teaching practice. Before we move to this exercise, however, it is helpful to think for a moment about what the LCPs mean as a whole—that is, what do they help us understand as we attempt to educate the whole learner, child through adolescent.

One of the biggest issues teachers face in our journey to becoming learner centered is challenging all students to learn to their highest levels. With the

increasing diversity in today's classrooms and schools, this is a huge challenge. Nonetheless, we believe that deeply understanding the LCPs and the nature of human learning, motivation, and development—regardless of student differences in race, culture, socioeconomic background, family situations, and academic backgrounds—provides us with the hope and the knowledge necessary to address this challenge. While it is true that most schools are faced with attempting to address the achievement gap in the performance of some children (usually between poor and/or minority youth and affluent and/or white youth), they have not adequately addressed balancing the academic curriculum with nonacademic curriculum and experiences that address the needs of the whole learner.

There are also many other factors outside school that need to be part of the solution, including family and community systems. One of the biggest factors responsible for the achievement gap is poverty (Berliner, 2005). Because poverty is a function of social and economic policies, schools cannot be blamed. In fact, Berliner argues that doing reform outside of school to help reduce the social and economic gap will be more effective than reform within the schools. Because achievement is consistently correlated with poverty, increasing the income of the poor and teaching good nutrition, high quality child care, good medical care and insurance, and quality summer programs together promise to have the biggest payoff in terms of helping to raise achievement. Further complicating factors are that the poorest children attend the oldest schools with the highest levels of lead poisoning. Teachers and other educators are left with the dilemma of how to maximize the effectiveness of what they do with students while they are in schools that present problems because of their age, funding, locations, and level of community support. This is where learner-centered principles and practices can provide sound support and guidelines for addressing the needs of the whole learner.

To enhance academic performance, more than good instruction is necessary. Studies are showing that lack of peer acceptance is related to declines in academic performance (Flock et al., 2005). Conversely, teachers

acting as mentors and forming strong relationships with their students are related to improved academic performance (Murray & Malmgren, 2005). Other studies show that rigorous, standards-based curriculum and strong social support systems that include people who value students and their learning are successful practices that reduce the achievement gap (Gordon, 2004). For success in urban schools, in particular, promoting a positive culture—caring connections between teachers and students, positive behavioral supports, and teaching social and emotional skills—is essential for students to reach high achievement levels (Osher & Fleischman, 2005).

The role of educators and schools in helping to offset growing youth problem behaviors has been the focus of recent research. There appears to be agreement that coordinated, long-term, and systemic efforts are required— those that address family, school, and community (Weissberg et al., 2003). Statistics from the U.S. Department of Health and Human Services show that as many as 20% of children and adolescents experience mental disorders and more than 80% of these receive no services. Thirty percent of 14- to 17-year-olds engage in multiple high-risk behaviors and another 35% in medium-risk problem behaviors. There is now recognition that a focus on health rather than illness and on prevention rather than treatment will have the most positive long-term results. Current efforts to produce long-term results involve bringing prevention researchers and practitioners together to develop programs based on health and prevention (Biglan et al., 2003).

With increased national emphasis on evidence-based practices, however, some educators are arguing that there are no clear interventions at the community level that can be demonstrated to be effective (Wandersman & Florin, 2003), while others contend effective prevention and intervention programs can be developed (Nation et al., 2003). For instance, Nation et al. found a number of characteristics that were consistently related to effective prevention approaches:

- The programs were comprehensive.
- They included varied teaching methods.
- They were of sufficient frequency and duration.
- They were theory driven.
- They provided opportunities for positive relationships.
- They were appropriately timed.
- They were socioculturally relevant.
- They included outcome evaluation.
- They involved well-trained staff.

One of the most effective models involved the creation of caring communities of learners and the enhancement of school and classroom climate (Greenberg et al., 2003). Such enhancements include strategies that emphasize student involvement in class meetings, peer leadership, family involvement, and whole-school community building activities, all of which help to build trust and support. The program described by Greenberg et al. utilized these strategies, which reflect one or more of the LCPs and are consistent with the LCM, in combination with helping youth to develop essential academic and nonacademic skills and school staff to develop personal and organizational change. Another model that follows the LCPs, described by Kelley, Mills, and Shuford (2005), uses a principle-based approach to school violence prevention. In their approach, they suggest that educators deal directly with the root causes of school violence (i.e., poor mental health of youth who are at risk). In this approach, teachers and others directly educate youth about mental functioning, and youth themselves can take responsibility for recapturing positive mental health in terms of well-being, self-esteem, common sense, positive motivation, and other healthy attributes of positive youth development. Research by Kelley et al. demonstrates that this approach can lead to marked improvement in the mental health of youth which, in turn, leads to a significant reduction in school violence.

The box on the next page illustrates how one teacher can have a positive, powerful influence on students who are at risk for violent behavior. The moral of the story is significant in that it concerns the benefits of the learner-centered principles that factor so prominently in all effective programs, not to mention in everyday life. What makes the story more compelling is that it describes the real experience of one of the authors (McCombs). It is an example that underlines the ability of the learner-centered principles to instill order, focus, discipline, and motivation even in schools (or natural "living systems," as many researchers now term these environments) that are beset by student gangs, crime, and intimidation.

The Math Class Story

This story originated in a Colorado middle school that was working with me on a project titled "Neighbors Making a Difference." This project was aimed at fostering positive relationships between teachers and their students (as well as between students and other meaningful adults in their immediate community), as a strategy for offsetting student gang involvement and drug use. Many of the teachers at this middle school, however, had expressed fear of these "tough" students as well as the view that there was little they could do to reach them. I decided to spend a day at the school and become a witness to what was happening in the classroom for both students and teachers. I simply sat unobtrusively in the backs of classrooms, following a group of students throughout their class periods in order to get a closer look at the governing dynamics in the relationships between the ill-reputed students and their struggling teachers.

After the experience, when I was talking with some colleagues, I somewhat wryly remarked that I was "amazed [the students] weren't schizophrenic." What I meant was that observing a variety of different classes throughout the day was like an "up and down roller coaster," with students in classes taught by learner-centered teachers behaving wonderfully, in stark opposition to the students in classes with non-learner-centered teachers. To top it off, I was even witness to a student fight in the hallway right before a final period math class, which apparently was not an atypical experience for these middle school pupils. I couldn't help but wonder to what length such students would go to disrupt the traditionally unfavorable subject of math, particularly as it was at the end of a long school day.

To my great surprise, however, as the students filed into the class, I was privy to a quite surreal, yet inspiring display. Without even the prominent presence of a teacher or authority figure, the students immediately became quiet and self-disciplined, picking out the appropriate materials from folders positioned along the side of the classroom, sitting down at their desks, pairing up into pre-set groups to work on their current computer projects, and promptly beginning to work without even the slightest command or provocation from a teacher.

Curious as to the whereabouts of the teacher, I finally noticed the teacher kneeling to find some reference materials in the back of the room. A student walked back to ask him a question, and that was when it became obvious that he was the teacher. From that point on, he periodically walked around and checked student work already in progress. Clearly, I realized, there was much to be learned from this teacher and his seemingly effortless style in facilitating a self-directed learning process for the students. After witnessing several teachers desperately trying to control their students in rowdy and unruly classroom settings, here was a teacher that trusted students to be self-regulated and self-motivated. And that's what was happening. Not only was the teacher freed from keeping his students in control, he also was able to support and engage students in meaningful assignments. The result was positive motivation bereft of any student disturbances or complaints.

After the math class was over, I couldn't resist asking the teacher how he had achieved such an impressive feat—particularly so in light of my previous experiences at the school. The teacher explained his philosophy about the natural desire to learn in all students and the events that led to his successful classroom environment. At the beginning of the year, the teacher said, he simply and directly told the students, "This is your class. We can do it any way you want as long you learn the math." In other words, while the teacher did lay out his "non-negotiables"—the essential elements necessary to cover content standards and to ensure that the work got done—he largely left the options and details up to his students. Apparently, in leaving many of the choices and the rules for how the class should be managed up to his students, the teacher had gained their respect and concentration. Most importantly, he met students' needs to have some choice and control—he instilled the ownership that allowed them to take responsibility for their own learning. He relayed that not only were students harder on themselves in setting up classroom rules than he would have been, but because they felt ownership, it was their class and they enforced the rules. His job was easier and he had helped instill in the students a sense of responsibility and motivation that transcended everything except their desire to learn. This experience culminated in the inspiration for a book, published by the American Psychological Association, that I wrote with this wise teacher, titled *Motivating Hard-to-Reach Students.*

Developmental research on risk and resilience demonstrates the power of a close bond with at least one adult as well as support from caring communities. The research on human development and the best practices of those working with an ecological or living systems perspective indicates that classroom ecosystems need to attend to the psycho-social-physical needs of children and youth. Specifically, classrooms need to be healthy places to learn and to help students become successful academically and interpersonally. Healthy classrooms

- help students see themselves as competent and effective learners,
- encourage self-determination by having students set their own learning goals,
- support students in becoming self-controlled by behaving adaptively with a minimum of adult supervision,
- focus on caring and authentic relationships between students and teachers,
- foster ongoing and rewarding friendships with classmates, and build positive home-school connections to help families know

how to strengthen learning that occurs in the classroom.

These practices draw heavily on research related to the LCPs as well as McCombs's (1999a, 2000a, 2001, 2003a, 2004b, in press) ongoing research on what constitutes evidence-based learner-centered practices.

Now it is time for you to put on your most reflective "thinking cap." To help you reflect on what the 14 LCPs mean to you, we have created an exercise (Exercise 4.1) that allows you to put into words your thoughts and ideas about them. Exercise 4.2 helps you decide what "learner centered" is and is not.

What's Next?

In Chapter 5, we focus on how to apply the learner-centered principles to teaching practices. In the context of Glasser's six conditions for quality schoolwork as they apply to the use of learner-centered practices, we discuss classroom climate, the relevance of learner-centered practices in the context of standards and assessment, and ways to address low achievement.

Exercise 4.1

Thoughts and Feelings About the LCPs

Metacognitive and Cognitive Factors

What do these principles mean to you in your practice? In other words, how do the principles manifest themselves in your classroom?

- Learning is a natural process
- Learning is personal constructions of meaning
- Learning is relating personal meanings to shared knowledge
- Learning is facilitated by higher-order thinking processes
- Learning is facilitated by environmental factors, including culture, technology, and instructional practices

Motivational and Affective Factors

What do these principles mean to you in your practice? In other words, how do the principles manifest themselves in your classroom?

- Motivation is a function of internal beliefs, values, interests, expectations, emotions, states of mind
- Motivation to learn is a natural process when beliefs and emotions are positive and when external context is supportive
- Motivation-enhancing tasks facilitate higher-order thinking and learning processes as a function of perceived relevance and meaningfulness as well as optimal difficulty and novelty

Developmental and Social Factors

What do these principles mean to you in your practice? In other words, how do the principles manifest themselves in your classroom?

- Learning is influenced by unique genetic and environmental factors
- Learning is facilitated by developmentally appropriate experiences and materials
- Developmental differences encompass physical, intellectual, emotional, and social areas
- Learning is influenced by social interactions, interpersonal relations, and communication with others

Individual Differences Factors

What do these principles mean to you in your practice? In other words, how do the principles manifest themselves in your classroom?

- The same basic principles of learning apply to all individuals
- Learners differ in learned and genetic "preferences" for how they learn
- Individuals' unique perceptions, learned beliefs, and prior learning experiences provide a "filter" for learning new information and interpreting "reality"
- Setting appropriately high and challenging standards and assessing the learner and learning progress are integral parts of the learning process

Exercise 4.2

What Is Learner-Centered and What Is Not Learner-Centered?

Under the "not" column, list what you think contrasts with each item in the "is" column. Can you think of examples in your classroom of any of the items you list in the "not" column? If so, how might you change them so they would fit better under the "is" column?

LEARNER-CENTERED IS	LEARNER-CENTERED IS NOT
• a research-based framework	_____
• focused on well-defined content	_____
• standards and learning	_____
• objectives	_____
• a balance of teacher and student	_____
• control	_____
• a balance of learner and learning	_____
• needs	_____
• concerned with high levels of	_____
• learning and motivation	_____
• rigorous and challenging	_____
• shared teacher and student	_____
• responsibility for learning	_____

5

Learner-Centered Practices

As our journey now takes us deeper into what the LCPs mean for teaching and learning, we invite you to first consider carefully some core questions regarding your own beliefs, values, and philosophies. We have discovered that responding to these questions is a necessary first step in becoming learner centered. Our questions have been borrowed from Ferrero (2005), who claims that what characterizes high-performing schools are the beliefs and values of educators. These lead to diverse practices that, in turn, lead to school excellence. The "one size fits all" metaphor simply does not make schools great. In Ferrero's look at seven great high schools, he found that they *all* worked to produce students who are good citizens, caring people, critical thinkers, and productive contributors to the economy. Although the specific practices, programs, and policies varied from school to school, the teachers and administrators in all seven schools shared two common traits. They believed learning should be relevant to students, and they were willing to be guided by value judgments as well as research and theory.

Because beliefs and values are fundamental to creating learner-centered practices, we invite you to reflect on and journal your responses to the questions raised by Ferrero (2005). As you think through and respond to the questions, consider how you can become part of creating a great school through the development of coherent learning communities.

- What motivated me to go into teaching?
- What do I think students should know and be able to do?
- Who are the influences on my education philosophy?
- Which colleagues share my vision?
- What do parents, students, and local citizens want, need, and believe?

After you have read this chapter of suggested practices, we invite you to return to the responses you entered in your journal, compare them with the ideas and practices we describe in this chapter, and talk with your colleagues about what you are learning and how your learning is affecting your teaching practices.

Turning Principles Into Practices

One of the strongest implications of the LCP and LCM is that education must address the whole learner. This is certainly not a new idea. Although many educators have advocated for holistic education models (e.g., Combs, 1986, 1991; Noddings, 2005), the evidence base for this approach was less clear in earlier years than it is now. Making the case even stronger for positive outcomes that extend beyond academic achievement, Noddings (2005) argues that schools were established as much for moral and social reasons as for academic instruction; that is, they were established to serve both individuals and the larger society. This means that we, as a society, want not only competent workers but graduates with sound character; social conscience; the ability to think critically; and awareness of global situations, problems, and approaches to solutions.

Noddings (2005) argues that to sustain our democracy, schools need to help develop thoughtful citizens who can make wise civic choices. Eisner (2005) points out that current policy focused on clear outcomes defined by measurable standards is highly rational with impeccable logic because it allows us to measure performance and hold schools and teachers accountable. However, the problem with this policy is that it narrows the vision of

education so that it addresses only intellectual capacities, neglecting the social and emotional qualities of students, teachers, families, and communities. It promotes a technical rather than organic, humanistic, or personal orientation to teaching that does not work well with living beings. Eisner argues that we need to return to the vision of progressive education articulated by Dewey (1938) that recognized distinctive talents of individual children and created environments to actualize those potentialities. Returning to this vision means that teachers should design experiences that allow students to respond not just in cognitive ways, but also emotionally, imaginatively, and socially. It also means that assessment should focus on more than academic outcomes and also include the other more formative measures of what best nourishes the whole child. The basic argument for the education of the whole child is that in human organisms, there are no independent parts; all are interconnected and work in an ongoing synchrony (Eisner, 2005). When instructional practices are fragmented and address only one domain of human functioning during learning, the result is that learners feel disconnected and alienated from the process. Their motivation to learn suffers, and negative attitudes form toward both learning and schooling.

Given the need for holistic education and because of the uniqueness of each human being, Kohn (2005) argues that we need to accept individual children for who they are rather than what they do. To do otherwise, that is, to expect all children to learn the same things in the same way and at the same rate, runs the risk of valuing some capabilities more than others. Particularly when teachers are under pressure to raise scores on a narrow curriculum of math and reading, the students who do well in those areas are frequently valued more than the students who do poorly in those areas. Children then get the message that their worth is conditional on their performance. Further, they learn that they are acceptable, both to themselves and to others, only under certain conditions—a situation that leads these students to several possibilities:

- pretending to be someone teachers and parents will love,
- acting out,
- leaving school,
- developing physical symptoms related to stress,
- developing mental health problems.

Kohn (2005) cites research that indicates that when students feel unconditionally accepted by their teachers, they are more interested in learning and enjoy challenging tasks more compared to students whose support from teachers is conditional. Learner-centered teachers understand the value of addressing the needs of the whole child or learner by using unconditional teaching practices that accept the whole learner and the uniqueness of his or her background, talents, and interests.

Williams (2003) points out that decades of research into human resilience and student performance document the power of addressing the whole learner by providing caring teachers and schools. The power is in the results that such practices achieve— the development of young people who can successfully overcome risks and challenges. Caring teachers can make the difference between students at risk for failure and students who possess resilience and the ability to learn. Caring and learner-centered teachers convey high expectations and provide opportunities for students to be active participants in their own learning process, providing not only opportunities for students to achieve academic skills, but also a confident and positive model for character development. Caring teachers are compassionate, interested in, actively listen to, and get to know the gifts and talents of individual students (Williams, 2003). They hold strong beliefs in all students' innate resilience and capacity to learn.

The fundamental characteristic of schools that can make the difference between risk and resilience is the quality of relationships between teachers and students—a hallmark and foundation of the learner-centered classroom and school. With a focus on relationships, these schools build small learning communities in which students' needs to belong are met. In urban schools, in particular, great teachers believe it is their job to make sure that all students succeed (Corbett, Wilson, & Williams, 2005). Corbett et al. conducted a three-year study of teachers in two urban school districts. Although these great teachers use a variety of best practices—cooperative groups, checking for understanding, hands-on activities, connecting new content to prior knowledge, and other strategies consistent with the LCPs—it was their attitudes that really made the difference in helping students succeed. When students were asked about these teachers, they indicated they like teachers who use strict approaches and high expectations because they know these teachers care and want them to have a good education.

These great teachers studied by Corbett et al. (2005) also give students considerable responsibility to make choices and participate in meaningful activities. Their results show what we consistently find with learner-centered practices: successful schools—great schools—aren't about the practices alone; they're also about the beliefs, attitudes, and characteristics of teachers that provide the support for all students to succeed. We'll say more about this a bit later. Our next step is to take a look at what practices lead students to the quality outcomes we value.

Glasser's Six Conditions for Quality Schoolwork

For decades, educators and researchers have argued that the basic approach to education should be one that strives to meet unique and fundamental human needs (Patterson, 2003). For example, William Glasser (1984, 1990), the originator of choice theory and Quality Schools, maintains that until we create more need-satisfying schools, we will not have more motivated students who work harder and learn more, and we will not have lower dropout rates. When schools are more personalized and need-satisfying rather than aimed at controlling students, we will be able to avoid tragedies such as the violence at Columbine High School. Personalized, need-satisfying schools provide environments in which students can really get to know their peers and teachers and develop a sense of trust in themselves and in their school as a community in which everyone has multiple and varied opportunities to explore and learn. When the focus is primarily on standards, covering the curriculum, and high-stakes testing, students know the system isn't about them.

It is essential that students have opportunities to become self-directed as they study real-world problems and learn in order to understand. Describing what he calls the new school paradigm, Patterson (2003) argues that decisions will be made based on what makes educational and personal sense for students rather than on administrative and teacher convenience or tradition. We believe that the type of new school paradigm that is needed is based on the evidence that has accumulated regarding the psychological principles of learning, motivation, development, and individual differences. From within this paradigm, students can develop into the critical thinkers, self-directed learners, problem solvers, time managers, and lifelong learners needed in our complex and rapidly evolving society. As Darling-Hammond (1997) puts it, despite decades of school reform efforts, we still structure schools in the mechanistic factory model/assembly line paradigm that was a product of the theories of behaviorism and reductionism popular in the 20th century.

Moreover, as Bracey (2002) argues, current reform strategies are

- superficial and fragmented, limited to improving individual achievement while increasing gaps between groups,
- lacking in theoretical coherence, and
- inadequate to define or address current educational and social challenges.

Drawing from Glasser's (1994) work, Bracey (2002) outlined six conditions that must be in place in the classroom for students to do quality work. We cite these conditions here because they align perfectly with what it means to be learner centered. These six conditions are also described in more detail in McCombs and Whisler (1997, pp. 85–56).

1. *There must be a warm, supportive classroom environment.* We, as teachers, must allow students to get to know us and, it is to be hoped, like us. Glasser points out that we work harder for those we know and like.

2. *Students are asked to do only useful work.* And teachers must explain the usefulness of what they are asking students to do. We teach information if it is directly related to a life skill, if students express a desire to learn it, if we teachers believe it is especially useful, or if it is required for college.

3. *Students are always asked to do the best they can do.* The conditions of quality work include students

   – knowing us as teachers and appreciating that we have provided a caring place to work,

   – believing the work assigned is always useful,

   – being willing to put a great deal of effort into their work, and

   – knowing how to evaluate and improve upon their work.

4. *Students are asked to evaluate their own work.* Because self-evaluation is a prerequisite to quality work, teachers must teach all students to

   – evaluate their own work,

   – improve it based on that evaluation, and

   – repeat this process until quality has been achieved.

5. *Quality work always feels good.* Students feel good when they produce quality work, and so do their parents. We teachers feel happy as we observe this process. Glasser believes that it is feeling good that is the incentive to pursue quality.

6. *Quality work is never destructive.* Quality is never achieved by doing something destructive such as doing drugs (even though that may produce good feelings) or harming people, property, the environment, and the like. When students "own" the quality of their work, teachers observe how this extends beyond quality academic work to quality of personal and social outcomes.

Classroom Climate

For decades, the quality of the classroom climate has been noted as essential to promoting a positive learning environment. Because there are many aspects to classroom climate, researchers are beginning to understand that no two individuals will agree on exactly what the dimensions of climate entail. What is critical, however, is that students perceive that they are cared about, respected, in positive relationships with their teacher and their peers, and that it is safe to make mistakes (McCombs & Whisler, 1997).

The role of climate in supporting student development was revealed in a recent report from a special National Study Group for the Affirmative Development of Academic Ability (2004). This report crafted a vision for affirming academic ability, nurturing intellective competence, and moving all students to high levels of academic achievement. A particular focus was on minority and low-income students and the development of competencies that could eliminate the academic achievement gaps among various groups of children. Specific competencies addressed included literacy and numeracy, mathematical and verbal reasoning, problem solving, sensitivity to multiple contexts and perspectives, relationship skills, self-regulation, resource recognition and help-seeking, and skill in accessing and managing information.

The study group contended that "Affirmative development of academic ability is nurtured and developed through

- high-quality teaching and instruction in the classroom,
- trusting relationships in school, and
- supports for pro-academic behavior in the school and community." (p. 1)

The report described intellective competence as a holistic set of affective, cognitive, and situational mental processes that help learners make sense of their experiences and solve problems.

The Hay McBer (2000) report offers another learner-centered perspective on climate and how it affects learning. It identifies nine dimensions that we believe are crucial aspects of climate in a learner-centered classroom:

- clarity around the purpose of each lesson,
- order within the classroom,
- a clear set of standards,
- fairness,
- opportunities for active participation,
- support to try new things and learn from mistakes,
- emotional and physical safety,
- interesting and stimulating learning, and
- a comfortable and attractive physical environment.

We recommend a systemic approach to classroom, school, and community climate that incorporates the findings of the National Study Group for the Affirmative Development of Academic Ability (2004) and Hay McBer's (2000) nine dimensions. At the classroom level, we recommend inquiry-based approaches for helping all students acquire knowledge, followed by deep learning techniques such as reflection, journaling, and applications of what is being learned in complex real-world problems. We also recommend practice of basic skills and concepts until they become automatic. We further recommend authentic, naturalistic situations with a focus on collaborative learning and social interaction. Students should also be taught strategies for transferring what they are learning from one task to another through problem-based approaches that emphasize metacognitive strategies that provide students with experience in gaining insights into strategic knowledge and monitoring their own learning processes.

At the school level, we recommend an emphasis on building trusting relationships that reflect the diversity of the students, teachers, and staff in the school. At the family and community levels, we encourage teachers to contribute to building the supports necessary to promote the economic, health, and personal welfare of all—perhaps by establishing partnerships with local businesses, merchants, and agencies; developing community service projects; and devising strategies that provide education supports to students and their families. Throughout, the emphasis is on designing and building academic and support environments that reflect the LCM and the LCPs.

Using evidence collected in the UK, the Hay McBer (2000) report on teacher effectiveness also identified a set of factors that they use to describe effective teaching. Though only one specifically addresses classroom climate, all three factors contribute to the learning climate of the classroom:

Teaching skills:

- involving all students in the lesson,
- using differentiation appropriate to challenge all students in the class,
- using a variety of activities or learning methods,
- applying teaching methods appropriate to curriculum objectives, and
- using a variety of questioning techniques to probe students' knowledge and understanding.

In short, effective teachers set high expectations, are good at planning, use a range of assessment techniques to monitor student understanding, and have clear strategies for student management.

Professional characteristics:

- professionalism, including
  - challenging and supporting students,
  - expressing confidence in students and their learning abilities, and
  - creating trust and respect for others.

- types of thinking used and modeled, including
  - analytical and
  - conceptual.

- planning and setting expectations: encouraging and supporting students'
  - drive for improvement,
  - information seeking, and
  - initiative.

Leadership qualities:

- flexibility,
- holding people accountable,
- managing students,
- expressing and modeling a passion for learning,
- relating to others:
  - having a positive impact and influence,
  - demonstrating and encouraging teamwork, and
  - showing an understanding of others.

- focus on classroom climate

Perhaps one of the most telling indicators of classroom climate is students' perceptions of an ideal teacher.

The Hay McBer report (2000) includes these descriptions of how eighth-grade students define their ideal teacher:

Is kind

Is generous

Listens to you

Encourages you

Has faith in you

Keeps confidences

Likes teaching children

Likes teaching their subject

Takes time to explain things

Helps you when you're stuck

Tells you how you are doing

Allows you to have your say

Doesn't give up on you

Cares for your opinion

Makes you feel clever

Treats people equally

Stands up for you

Makes allowances

Tells the truth

Is forgiving

These students' descriptions provide a clear illustration that the qualities that make teachers effective and learner centered are more than their practices. Who teachers are—their qualities and characteristics that comprise an often-overlooked aspect of the learning climate—is as critical to being learner centered as the practices, programs, and strategies they use. Because this is the first step toward becoming learner centered, it is worth serious consideration. Take another look at the above list and rate yourself from 1 to 5 on these qualities, with 5 indicating strong adherence to these qualities and 1 indicating weak or no adherence to these qualities. If you are feeling especially brave, ask your students to also rate you on these qualities! Once they have done so, ask yourself what you could do to increase your score on each quality and then journal your thoughts and conclusions.

Relevance of Learner-Centered Practices in the Context of Standards and Assessment

Most teachers are under growing and relentless pressure to prepare students for high-stakes tests and to cover vast amounts of content. For many, this leaves little time for learner-centered practices such as student discussions, inquiry-based learning, and extracurricular activities. In addition, because of the large size and diversity of many high schools, teachers find it nearly impossible to get to know their students, many of whom teachers see as indifferent or ill-behaved (Tomlinson & Doubet, 2005). Tomlinson and Doubet present snapshots of four teachers who, in spite of these pressures, have found ways to connect with students and make learning personally relevant.

One teacher makes writing relevant to students by letting them write about themselves and their own experiences, following required content standards but letting students know she's teaching them and not just "covering material." To help them understand the golden age of literature, she asks students to describe golden ages in their own lives and uses their descriptors as a segue into what the golden age has meant in literature as a field.

Another teacher uses students' ideas and questions about biology to guide their learning of core concepts. They complete lab reports and other products that they choose from either a teacher-provided or a student-designed list. Students also can choose one of three tasks, such as researching their own questions (e.g., who discovered the nature of metabolism), to continue their learning outside of class. Instead of using a textbook, students are encouraged to find authentic and reputable information in print or on the Web. The teacher constructs exercises that arouse students' curiosity, such as analyzing the foods they're eating and burning and figuring out the caloric content. They also figure out their own Body Mass Index and carbohydrate intake. The instruction is not about coverage; it's about inquiry and community.

A geography teacher focuses on connecting students with important ideas and connecting with them by knowing them as individuals. The curriculum is focused on key concepts that encourage students to ask important "how" and "why" questions, such as how different land forms in their areas came to be or why their state has the boundaries it does. To make the curriculum comfortable for the kids, the teacher begins by establishing positive interpersonal relationships. Technology is integrated in interesting and challenging ways to explain the Earth's power in tornadoes and hurricanes. Because many students have difficulty completing homework at home, a place is provided in school.

A human anatomy and physiology teacher focuses on affection and respect by persistently expecting and demanding high-quality work. Students work in teams and are encouraged to form a community of learners. They learn democratic processes for working together and building an environment in which everyone feels safe. These processes include learning to listen to diverse perspectives and learning from one another. Students then feel safe to express their points of view without ridicule.

The Achievement Gap Issue

One of the biggest issues teachers face in their journey to becoming learner centered is that of challenging all students to learn at their highest levels, particularly given the increasing diversity in today's classrooms and schools. We have seen that by developing a thorough understanding of the LCPs and the nature of human learning, motivation, and development—regardless of student differences in race, culture, socioeconomic background, family situations, and academic backgrounds—teachers become able to meet this challenge with ease. Although it is true that most schools are faced with attempting to address the achievement gap in the performance of some children (usually between poor and/or minority youth and affluent and/or white youth), those who have been studying the achievement gap issue (e.g., Carey, 2003; Gordon, 2004; Grossman & Ancess, 2004; Taylor, 2003) can provide us with helpful guidance. Filtering this guidance through the lens of the LCP and LCM, we offer these recommendations:

Make sure students are provided with equal opportunity to learn, which does not mean treating them the same. Rather, providing students with equal opportunity to learn means that students from different ethnic, cultural, and socioeconomic groups may need different types of supports to enhance and develop their learning (Rodriguez, 2005). To know what type of supports your students need, you must adhere to the foundational principle of learner-centered practice: You must know your students individually and establish a positive relationship with each student. The strategies for developing this basic foundation of learner-centered practice are easier than you may imagine and are described in Chapter 6.

Take a multifaceted approach and remember that caring comes first. A multifaceted approach has three elements:

- building relationships with students;
- providing a curriculum that is challenging, rigorous, and standards-based; and
- holding all students to high standards. (Collins, 2005)

Because children in poverty or those who are racially or culturally different often experience isolation and ridicule in schools, it is also essential that teachers reach out and show they care as well as distinguish between a student's potential to learn and the learning a student brings to school and demonstrates on test scores (Williams, 2005).

Use every interaction with students to gain insight into and understanding of each student's learning strengths and needs. In spite of the busy and complex life of the classrooms, learner-centered teachers understand how important it is to get to know each student personally. Many children with difficult backgrounds become passive and withdrawn because

they don't believe teachers are going to allow them to use their strengths (Collins, 2005).

Support the learning of the whole child. Teachers and parents alike want children to develop their unique gifts and talents, as well as grow up to be productive citizens, lifelong learners, and people able to live rich and enjoyable lives. We contribute significantly to this goal by helping students identify their talents and develop as many as possible in order to become well-rounded individuals. One way to do this is to be sure children are educated about the importance of adequate physical activity, a balanced diet, and avoiding toxins such as alcohol and drugs (Satcher, 2005). Another is to teach students how to make healthy decisions and take constructive actions in conflict situations such as bullying and negative peer pressure (Sroka, 2005). A third is to work in partnership with students to design violence prevention strategies so they have a sense of ownership and responsibility for enforcing positive social interactions (McCombs, 1999a). Building community in the classroom and giving students responsibilities and a voice in decisions that affect them, their peers, their classroom, and school are all instrumental in educating children as whole human beings.

Renew yourself and find ways to nurture yourself. As our world speeds up and the demands for achievement and performance increase, classrooms and schools can become high pressure environments unless care is taken to ensure otherwise. One way to reduce pressure on ourselves and our students is to take care of ourselves in holistic ways. To do this, we need to become advocates for our own health and wellness programs, including physical activities and meditation to help reduce stress, and developing our own IEPs to improve our quality of life (Shechtman, 2005). Taking care of ourselves in this way has both direct and indirect effects on our students: direct in that we are modeling health for our students; and indirect in that when we feel nurtured, we have a greater capacity to demonstrate caring toward our students.

Combine rigorous curriculum with attention to the social environment. As students move through the K–12 system, the social supports they need in order to succeed expand and change. In addition to teachers who care about their academic success, students need committed parental involvement, a peer group that believes in and supports learning and education, and mentors who can provide students with opportunities for expanding their knowledge and skills (American Educational Research Association [AERA], 2004).

Use action research to build understanding about the nature of the achievement gap. Action research entails initiating and conducting school- and classroom-based studies that enable you to reflect systematically on your teaching and collect data that will answer your questions. It follows, then, that the most effective action research for addressing the achievement gap is that relevant to the students in your school. What you discover from your action research may not necessarily be applicable to other schools, depending on neighborhood and community characteristics. For instance, what works to reduce the gap in an urban school may be very different from what works in wealthy neighborhoods.

Consider collecting demographic data as well as interviewing or surveying students regarding their views about why they are or are not excelling (Grossman & Ancess, 2004). This type of data can lead you to understand more clearly that minority students suffer from racial isolation and feelings of inadequacy, both of which can become a self-fulfilling prophecy in systems that track courses such as math. For example, if students are in low-ability tracks, these students and their teachers label them as weak in math, but when tracking and ability grouping are eliminated, they are helped to develop trusting relationships and self-confidence in their abilities to succeed. Figure 5.1 shows a survey used by a high school teacher to learn more about his students.

What Students Say About the Achievement Gap

Taylor (2003) asked African American high school students what they considered the reasons for their low achievement on national achievement tests. These students responded as follows:

- 31% held themselves responsible and said they could have applied themselves more and tried harder, but many were embarrassed to ask teachers for help.
- 24% said there were a variety of teacher factors involved, such as not getting much support from their teacher, the teacher not teaching the right thing or making learning fun or interesting, and/or having to do the same work in high school as elementary school.

(Text continues on page 85)

Figure 5.1   Student Awareness Survey

Johnson's Awareness Quotient

Name _____   Year in school _____

Siblings

Names and ages _____

_____

_____

Who I live with _____

Pets _____

Favorites

food _____

movie _____

music _____

restaurant _____

snack _____

TV show _____

Average hours per week I spend on academics/homework _____

Is there one night that seems more overloaded than others?_____

Favorite subjects and why

1. _____

2. _____

3. _____

Rank your skills from 1 to 10 (10 = highest) in the following areas

reading _____   athletics _____   creativity _____

writing _____   drama _____   visual arts _____

speaking _____   time mgmt _____   note taking _____

listening _____   friendship _____   musical arts _____

science _____   leadership _____   independence _____

math _____   interdependence _____

Extracurriculars I am currently involved in _____

_____

_____

Average time I spend per week _____

_____

_____

Extracurriculars I hope to be involved in this year _____

_____

_____

Average time I will spend per week_____

_____

Work

   where _____

   average hours per week _____

   responsibilities include _____

   When I have free time, I like to spend it with _____

   and/or by doing _____

I'd rather spend free time with my friends ___ or alone ___ Why? _____

_____

_____

Community services I'm involved with_____

_____

_____

(Continued)

Figure 5.1 (Continued)

Volunteering I do _____

_____

_____

Family obligations_____

_____

_____

Anything else that occupies your time? Share_____

_____

_____

Any post–high school plans_____

if college, ideas for major _____

if work, what field _____

if other, explain _____

Current course schedule _____

EB _____   Teacher _____

1st _____   Teacher _____

2nd_____   Teacher _____

3rd _____   Teacher _____

4th _____   Teacher _____

5th _____   Teacher _____

6th _____   Teacher _____

7th _____   Teacher _____

8th _____   Teacher _____

9th _____   Teacher _____

- 18% said the parents' role was critical and that many parents didn't get involved with what their kids were doing or help with homework, many held low expectations for their children, and many didn't spend enough time with them or discipline them enough.
- 13% felt school was a "joke" and didn't see the need for a high school diploma because it wouldn't help them get a job that paid enough; as a result, they didn't take state and national tests seriously but were not aware of what the world was saying about them in terms of their scores and the achievement gap.
- 11% said their community environment was a factor in terms of drugs and crime and they saw this environment as a trap because if they tried to leave their community they would be labeled as "acting white." Some were influenced by being able to make a lot of money on the streets, but the majority felt the streets were a bad influence on them.

The major recommendations from this study were that kids need to be involved each year in conversations similar to the one Taylor (2003) held with them, and that teachers need to gain more understanding about learning, human growth, child development, and the importance of culture.

Support for these recommendations comes from others who have studied the achievement gap problem, including Valencia, Valenzuela, Sloan, and Foley (2001). They contend that a primary reason underlying the achievement gap is a lack of equal educational opportunity, including inferior schools and lower-quality education. Carey (2003) reports that low-income, minority, and low-achieving students are disproportionately assigned to under-qualified, ineffective, and inexperienced teachers—leading to more low achievement for those students struggling the most to meet No Child Left Behind (NCLB) requirements. When these students are given more effective teachers, they show greater gains in reading and math. Carey (2003) cites evidence that having an above average teacher for five consecutive years can completely close the achievement gap between low-income students and others. What works, particularly with Latino youth, are more learner-centered practices that respect students' culture and language, involve parents and are sensitive to family circumstances, provide opportunities for youth to engage in self-directed learning and leadership opportunities, include youth and their voices in the process, and provide quality professional development opportunities.

Reflection

Have you or anyone in your school asked the students what they think are the reasons for low achievement? If so, how well do their responses match those we described in the previous section? If not, what do you think they would say? You may wish to design an interview form to use in collecting their views regarding the factors underlying low achievement. You may also wish to include questions designed to learn what the students believe are the factors contributing to high achievement.

What's Next?

In Chapter 6 we describe what the evidence shows about effective learner-centered practices in Grades K–3 and 4–12. We explore the relationship between "classroom management" and learner-centered practices, and we discuss evidence-based strategies for creating learner-centered, resilient classrooms.

6

Effective Learner-Centered Practices

In our more than 15 years of research-ing which practices are consistent with the APA Learner-Centered Psycho-logical Principles, we have discovered the most effective types of practice for students in Grades K–3 and for students in Grades 4–12.

Effective Learner-Centered Practices for Students in K–3

In our research with young children in Kindergarten through Grade 3, we have found three domains of practice to be most relevant to their highest levels of achievement and motivation (Daniels, Kalkman, & McCombs, 2001; McCombs, Perry, & Daniels, in press; Perry & Weinstein, 1998). We use a pyramid (Figure 6.1) to show the rela-tionship of these three types of practice, beginning with the most important, Establishing Positive Relationships and a Positive Climate for Learning. The second most important is Provide

Motivational Support for Learning, and the third is Facilitate Students' Thinking and Learning Skills.

Specific practices for teaching young children include

1. Establishing Positive Relation-ships and a Positive Climate for Learn-ing. Teacher practices in this domain focus on helping students feel that they are cared about and they belong, and helping them to feel good about them-selves and to get along with their class-mates. These practices include fostering a caring personal relationship with each student, helping students learn how to create caring personal relation-ships with their peers, and helping students value their unique abilities.

2. Providing Motivational Support for Learning. Teacher practices in this domain focus on helping students iden-tify their learning interests and unique talents, learn how to collaborate and work with their classmates on projects, and develop good listening and talking

Figure 6.1 Practices Aligned With the *Learner-Centered Psychological Principles* (APA, 1997) for Early Elementary School Levels

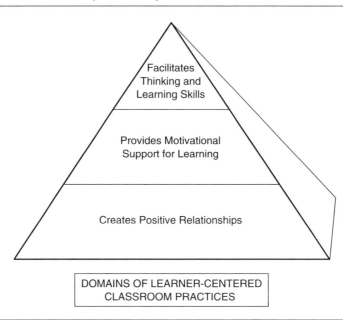

Facilitates Thinking and Learning Skills

Provides Motivational Support for Learning

Creates Positive Relationships

DOMAINS OF LEARNER-CENTERED CLASSROOM PRACTICES

skills. Included in this area of practice are teachers asking students what they like to learn about and their favorite ways of learning, and helping students see the value of making mistakes and learning how to tackle difficult learning challenges.

3. Facilitating Students' Thinking and Learning Skills. Teacher practices in this domain focus on helping students learn strategies for understanding what they are learning, remembering important information, and managing their time while working on assignments. Other practices include assisting students with difficult work that is hard for them, helping students think hard, and showing them how to do their work in better ways.

In our research leading to the validation of these practices, we found that young children can reliably and validly distinguish learner-centered from non-learner-centered teachers (McCombs et al., in press). Those students with learner-centered teachers not only achieved at higher levels but were also more motivated and engaged in the learning process. In contrast, young children with non-learner-centered teachers were already exhibiting signs of withdrawing from learning, disruptive classroom behavior, and lower levels of achievement. Combined with the results on students in Grades 4–12, these findings show clearly how learner-centered classrooms contribute to positive student outcomes.

Effective Learner-Centered Practices for Students in Grades 4–12

There are four types of practice that apply to students in Grades 4–8 and 9–12 and that our research has shown are strongly related to a range of student outcomes, including

- classroom achievement standardized test scores in reading and math,
- motivation to learn,
- lifelong learning skills,
- attendance, and
- classroom behavior. (Deakin Crick & McCombs, in press; McCombs, 2001, 2004a; Meece, Herman, & McCombs, 2003; Perry & Daniels, 2004; Pierce, Holt, Kolar, & McCombs, 2004)

These four types of practice, which we think of as domains of practice, are to be distinguished from the domains characterizing schools as living systems and the domains of the Learner-Centered Principles that we described in Chapter 2. To refresh your memory, the box below lists the two sets of domains from Chapter 2 so you can compare them

with the domains of practice we are discussing here.

As we did with the most effective types of practice for students in Grades K–3, in Figure 6.2 we used a pyramid to illustrate the relationship of the four domains of practice to the specific student outcomes we listed above. That is, the type of practice shown by the evidence to be the most important to positive student outcomes is the one on the bottom of the pyramid, Creating Positive Interpersonal Relationships and a Positive Climate for Learning. The type of practice shown to be the second most important to positive student outcomes is the one just above the bottom level of the pyramid, Honoring Student Voices and Providing Personal Challenge. The third most important is Encouraging Higher-Order Thinking and Self-Regulation. Finally, the fourth most important is Adapting to Individual Developmental Differences.

Our research has demonstrated that from the students' perspectives, if they feel connected to their teachers and that they are in a positive learning environment, if they feel their voice is listened to and respected and they are personally challenged, if they feel their higher-order thinking and learning

---

Domains of Schools as Living Systems and Domains of Learner-Centered Principles Described in Chapter 2

Domains of Schools as Living Systems	Domains of the Learner-Centered Principles
Personal	Cognitive and metacognitive
Technical	Motivational and affective
Organizational	Developmental and social
	Individual differences

Figure 6.2 Practices Aligned With the *Learner-Centered Psychological Principles* (APA, 1997) for Middle and High School Levels

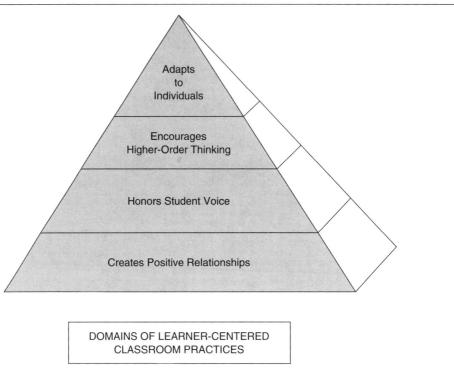

DOMAINS OF LEARNER-CENTERED
CLASSROOM PRACTICES

skills are supported, they feel their teachers are able to make adaptations for them as individuals. That is not to say that teachers needn't engage in other individualization strategies, but to be learner centered, teachers don't start there. They start with the domain of practice shown to be the most important for positive student outcomes and systematically address each of the other three domains of practice in turn.

1. Creating Positive Interpersonal Relationships and Climate. Teacher practices in this domain focus on the positive interpersonal and learning climate factors that help students feel respected, cared about and appreciated as individuals, that they belong, and that they are in a safe environment for learning. These practices include fostering a caring personal relationship with each student, helping students learn how to create caring personal relationships with their peers, and helping students value their unique abilities.

When educators care about student learning and about them as individuals, students feel connected to the academic environment (Blum, 2005). By the time students reach high school, about half of them report they do *not* believe that adults care about their learning or about them as individuals. According to Blum (2005), this finding brings up the larger question of what educators can do to reconnect with their students, especially at the high school level, where it is even more important for students to feel connected if they are to make healthy choices. Blum's research indicates that there are three school characteristics that help students feel connected to the school and feel challenged academically:

a. high academic standards combined with strong teacher support,

b. positive and respectful adult and student relationships, and

c. a school environment that is physically and emotionally safe.

These qualities define learner-centered schools, which research consistently shows produce students who are much more likely to have a range of positive outcomes in addition to high academic achievement and the motivation to stay in school and to graduate (McCombs, 2003a, 2004b). Gordon's work (2004) has shown that the combination of rigorous, standards-based curriculum and strong social support systems, including people who value students and their learning, significantly reduces the achievement gap. For success in urban schools, in particular, promoting a positive culture is essential, including caring connections, positive behavioral supports, and teaching social and emotional skills (Osher & Fleischman, 2005).

Along with teachers' abilities to create safe and caring learning communities at the classroom level, a positive classroom culture matters more than class size. Giving students choice and responsibility, using cooperative learning strategies, and recognizing student progress are all practices that create a positive classroom culture (Blum, 2005). Crabtree (2004) also reports that students respond best to teachers who are allowed to be highly creative and passionate, build strong relationships with students, and tailor the learning process to individual student needs.

2. **Honoring Student Voice, Encouraging Perspective-Taking, and Providing Personal Challenge.** Teacher practices in this domain focus on providing opportunities for students to express their perspectives while learning and listening to the perspectives of other students. These practices also include encouraging students to challenge and think for themselves while learning, as well as helping students express their uniqueness, develop personal responsibility for their own learning, and learn to understand multiple perspectives.

Enhancing academic performance requires more than good teaching. For instance, we know that lack of peer acceptance is related to declines in academic performance (Flock, Repetti, & Ullman, 2005). We also know that having teachers as mentors and engaging in strong student-teacher relationships are both related to improved academic performance (Murray & Malmgren, 2005).

One approach that is receiving renewed attention as a means of increasing positive student outcomes, thus reducing the achievement gap, is the use of various sorts of games. For instance, Jenkins (2005) believes that good games motivate students to develop basic competencies and enter even more specialized areas of knowledge. Used not as a replacement for good teaching but as a tool to engage students, games let students take charge of their learning and make them conscious of their learning process by presenting challenges that they must work through. Other qualities of games listed by Jenkins (2005) are that

- they lower the threat of failure because you can try again;
- they foster a sense of engagement through immersion and having some stake in the events;
- they allow early success by presenting challenges but not overwhelming students;
- they link learning goals and what students need to do to achieve these goals;
- they create a social context that connects students to others who share their interests;
- they are multimodal and include not only multimedia but also ask students to assume multiple roles and perspectives; and
- they support mastery of new skills through rehearsal and seeking out additional information.

3. **Encouraging Higher-Order Thinking and Self-Regulation.** Teacher practices in this domain focus on providing opportunities that encourage students to develop higher-order thinking and learning strategies that can help them regulate and direct their learning processes. These practices include helping students relate materials to their interests and make learning more personally relevant, providing students with choice and control over their learning process to develop personal responsibility for learning, and supporting students in acquiring skills for directing their learning.

Although most educators have a general understanding of how to promote the intellectual processes involved in learning, many of us are unsure how to help students acquire and use higher-order or metacognitive thinking and learning skills. Developmental psychologists have done much to help us understand how various mental abilities develop throughout childhood and adolescence (Fabes & Martin, 2003; Meece, 2002). Specifically, we know that students develop the ability to think about their own learning and thinking at different rates and that this process unfolds gradually throughout childhood and adolescence and into adulthood (Polloway, Miller, & Smith, 2004).

People who study complex brain functions in learning recommend three primary classroom conditions that foster "brain-friendly" strategies:

a. fostering a relaxed but challenging environment,

b. immersing students in complex experiences with a variety of challenges, and

c. providing opportunities for active processing of experiences out in the world. (Franklin, 2005)

Students' abilities to learn for understanding and link new ideas to existing ideas are facilitated in learner-centered classrooms in which students are involved in authentic problems, inquiry-oriented learning, and learning experiences that foster their sense of autonomy and responsibility. Acting as co-learners and facilitators, teachers draw on learners' unique talents, capacities, and experiences (Schuh, Wade, & Knupp, 2005). Teachers in learner-centered classrooms encourage open, divergent dialogue in which they are comfortable sharing their own learning and modeling their own experiences.

4. **Adapting to Individual Developmental Differences.** Teacher practices in this domain focus on adapting instruction to a range of individual differences in students' backgrounds, cultures, prior knowledge, preferences for learning, and development. These practices include focusing attention on getting to know individual students and their families, changing learning assignments when students appear to be failing, capitalizing on the learning community that has been built in the classroom, and using the resources of other students as peer tutors and mentors.

For thousands of schools in poor neighborhoods, student turnover is at crisis proportions. It is constant and rapid, presenting tremendous challenges to not only repeat topics but to maintain discipline. Some schools have learned successful approaches in spite of these challenges. Dillon (2004) reports that in one elementary school in Indianapolis, from a total of 295 students, 175 transferred in or out. Procedures that have been helpful for responding to turnover are to assign new students a buddy, give diagnostic tests to identify strengths and weaknesses, and prescribe special programs of study. Still, the job is difficult and new strategies are needed.

What Happened to "Classroom Management"?

The term "classroom management" carries a connotation of managing students in order to maintain an orderly classroom in which learning can take place without disruption. Teachers the world over express growing concern about managing what may often seem like disinterested and unruly students. A variety of classroom management programs are available for teachers, ranging from nearly total coercion and control to supporting students in their learning to be self-disciplined. Programs of this type focus on changing students, modifying their behaviors so that they conform to what is considered manageable.

From a learner-centered perspective, however, we have learned that the most effective long-term solution to classroom management is one that begins with teachers knowing their students and then partnering with them to co-create the most effective classroom management and discipline policies. Even very young children are capable of self-management when partnered with caring teachers. In this climate of trust, children of all ages will talk with their teachers about behavior problems and issues that they work together to solve.

Instead of "change the kid" strategies, Doll, Zucker, and Brehm (2004) propose changing the classroom through new kinds of strategies that encourage social and emotional development that is integrated into school, family, and community approaches. Research on human development and data from those working within the ecological or living systems perspective we described in Chapter 2 demonstrate that to be effective, classroom ecosystems need to attend to the psycho-social-physical needs of children and youth. This means that classrooms need to be healthy places to learn—places that help students become successful academically, intrapersonally, and interpersonally. Healthy classrooms

- help students see themselves as competent and effective learners,
- encourage self-determination by having students set their own learning goals,
- support students in becoming self-controlled by behaving adaptively with a minimum of adult supervision,
- focus on caring and authentic relationships between students and teachers,
- foster ongoing and rewarding friendships with classmates, and
- build positive home-school connections to help families know how to strengthen learning that occurs in the classroom. (McCombs, 1999a, 2000a, 2001, 2003b, 2004b, in press)

No doubt you recognize that the characteristics of healthy classrooms are virtually identical to learner-centered classrooms. This makes even more sense in light of one of the most alarming statistics in many schools: increased levels of bullying and violence. Although more severe forms of violence seem to be on the decline, various forms of aggressive peer behaviors and bullying are causing a growing number of high school students to skip school for fear of getting hurt (Yee, 2004). Further, it is highly likely that every regular education teacher will have at least one highly aggressive child in his or her classroom (Alvarez & Ollendick, 2004/2005). Another study found that nearly 7 in 10 middle and high school teachers have serious problems with students who disrupt classes (Carter, 2004).

The role of educators and schools in helping to offset growing youth problem behaviors has received considerable attention recently from researchers interested in learning how to address these problem behaviors. Most researchers agree that coordinated, long-term, and systemic efforts are required—those that address and include family, school, and community (Weissberg, Kumpfer, & Seligman, 2003). Statistics from the U.S. Department of Health and Human Services show that as many as 20% of children and adolescents experience mental disorders and more than 80% of these receive no services. Thirty percent of 14- to 17-year-olds engage in multiple high-risk behaviors and another 35% in medium risk problem behaviors (Weissberg et al., 2003). These statistics provide evidence that a focus on health rather than illness, and prevention rather than treatment, will have the most positive long-term results.

The best way to begin dealing with youth problem behaviors at the classroom level is to equip teachers with an understanding of the roots of aggressive and bullying behaviors. Teachers can use their increased knowledge and understanding of the causes of these behaviors to enlist their students as partners in developing team-based strategies for dealing with behaviors that are disruptive and that often lead to violence (McCombs, 1999a). And, as we said earlier, fostering caring and respectful relationships between students and teachers provides the basis for the sort of trust necessary for students and teachers to solve the difficult problems associated with bullying and violence.

Although some of those who study youth problem behaviors argue that there are no clear interventions at the community level that can be demonstrated to be effective (Wandersman & Florin, 2003), others contend that there are principles of effective prevention and intervention programs we can use to design and implement effective programs (Nation et al., 2003).

Current efforts are bringing prevention researchers and practitioners together to develop widespread implementation of evidence-based prevention practices that have been proven effective (Biglan, Mrazek, Carnine, & Flay, 2003). A number of characteristics are consistently related to the effective prevention approaches found in Nation et al.'s (2003) review. Effective prevention programs

- are comprehensive,
- include varied teaching methods,
- provide sufficient "dosage" (i.e., are intensive and/or frequent and/or long term),
- are theory driven,

- provide opportunities for positive relationships,
- are appropriately timed,
- are socioculturally relevant,
- include outcome evaluation, and
- involve well-trained staff.

Effective prevention programs have been developed by a variety of organizations and agencies, both public and private. The box below lists several empirically supported programs.

One of the most effective prevention models we recommend for your consideration creates caring communities of learners and enhances school and classroom climate (Greenberg et al., 2003). Strategies that emphasize student involvement in class meetings, peer leadership, family involvement, and whole school community-building activities help to build trust and

---

Empirically Supported Interventions That Prevent Drug Use, Violence, and HIV/AIDS

Centers for Disease Control and Prevention: www.cdc.gov/hiv/projects/rep/compend.htm

National Institute on Drug Abuse: www.nida.nih.gov/prevention/prevopen.html

Office of Juvenile Justice and Delinquency Prevention:

Blueprints for Violence Prevention Overview: www.colorado.edu/cspv/blueprints/index.html

Effective Family Programs for Prevention of DELINQUINCY: www.strengtheningfamilies.org

Youth Violence Message from the U.S. Surgeon General's Office: www.surgeongeneral.gov/library/youthviolence/report.html

U.S. Department of Education Office of Safe and Drug-Free Schools: http://www.ed.gov/about/offices/list/osdfs/programs.html

U.S. Department of Health and Human Services:

Effective programs and strategies: http://www.mentalhealth.samhsa.gov/youthviolence/surgeon general/SG_Site/chapter5/sec1.asp

Ineffective programs and strategies: http://www.mentalhealth.samhsa.gov/youthviolence/surgeon general/SG_Site/chapter5/sec6.asp

support. These strategies stem directly from the LCP and from research with the LCM and are combined with helping youth develop essential academic and nonacademic skills and effecting personal and organizational change among school staff. In addition, strategies based on the LCP directly address the root causes of school violence: the poor mental health of at-risk youth.

As teachers and other members of the learning community educate youth about mental functioning, the students themselves begin taking responsibility for recapturing positive mental health in terms of well-being, self-esteem, common sense, positive motivation, and other healthy attributes of positive development. Kelley, Mills, and Shuford (2005) have demonstrated that such an approach can lead to marked improvement in the mental health of youth, which, in turn, leads to a significant reduction in school violence. Similarly, Doll et al. (2004) report that classrooms exhibiting the characteristics of a resilient classroom demonstrate similar improvements in mental health, as well as reduction in school violence. The characteristics these classrooms share include

- academic efficacy—the belief in oneself as having control over one's academic success,
- behavioral self-control— knowledge and skills necessary for reflecting on and modifying one's behaviors,
- academic teacher-student relationships,
- effective peer relationships, and
- effective home-school relationships.

Each of these characteristics of resilient classrooms is supported and developed through classroom routines and practices specifically designed to strengthen each type of relationship.

Strategies for Creating Learner-Centered, Resilient Classrooms

Closely linked to involving students in self-directed strategies for classroom management are strategies that give students further voice and choice. Vaughn (2005), a high school Algebra I teacher with a high percentage of minority students with poor math backgrounds, faced a significant challenge to engage her students in assignments. She discovered that teaching her students to take control over their own learning through self-pacing dramatically raised their achievement. She realized the class needed to be redesigned to help students master skills sequentially at their own pace, in ways that allowed them to identify gaps in their knowledge and skills. She helped them set goals and plan their learning progress; they took exams when they were ready. Although she reported that her students hated the class at first, by the end of the semester they were saying, "I wish all my classes were like this" or "I learn better this way." Not only did their achievement increase, but discipline problems were rare.

Vaughn's experiences are echoed by Wolk (2005), who relates examples of high schools, notably Kennebunk High School in Maine, where students have a pronounced voice and participate in decision making on important matters. Not only is academic achievement improving, but students are learning democratic principles as well as the knowledge and skills they need to become productive, responsible citizens. They are participating in community projects of their choice and learning how to make a difference.

The Just for the Kids organization (2003) is showing in a series of national studies that the number one key to successful students and schools is to focus on the student, followed by high-quality teaching and evidence-based instructional practices. In successful schools, teachers are given the materials, training, and support they need and the time to plan together, discuss student progress, and reflect on best practices (Just for the Kids, 2003). In one such high-performance school in Los Angeles, teachers work together to help students take risks so that they develop character and the skills to succeed in life (Mathews, 2004a). Deborah Meier, who formed Central Park East School in East Harlem in 1974, found that the key to the success of the school and its students was the strong and educative or teaching/mentoring relationships between students and adults (Mathews, 2004b). Students were taught to develop their minds by weighing evidence, seeing other ways of looking at the same data or situation, comparing and contrasting, seeking patterns, conjecturing and arguing— skills that enabled them to use their minds powerfully (Meier, 2002). Current policies that do not teach students to engage in intellectual rigor and instead use their minds for factual recall will only add to the already growing dropout rate, particularly among disadvantaged and minority students (Wagner, 2003).

Comer (2005) maintains that the key to improving academic achievement is to link it to child and adolescent development. A school culture that promotes growth in physical, social, ethical, emotional, linguistic, and cognitive ways— that is, holistically—engages students in their entirety, thus reducing the probability that they will become bored, lost, angry, and/or disruptive. School cultures that ignore or resist what we know about child and adolescent development, especially the psychological principles of growth and health so basic to learning and achievement, risk student outcomes that fall far short of what we envision for the students we teach.

We know that cultures that promote belonging provide for comfort, confidence, competence, and motivation to learn. This has been verified in a number of programs for students at risk of high school dropout, such as the Denver program reported recently in the *Rocky Mountain News* ("Special Report," 2005), where a combination of academic rigor and personal approaches are showing success with Hispanic students. When Hispanic students in Denver describe their ideal high school, they say,

1. "We need new teachers. Teachers I can relate to. They'd be all black— like my mom. I can relate to my mom. Teach things I need to survive. They need more hands-on instead of sitting in class. I haven't been on a field trip since I've been here. We need a swimming pool. How come every other school has a swimming pool?" Michael, 15, freshman.

2. "In the ideal high school all students get treated fairly and

equally, and all get the same education whether they go to public school or private school. No student is allowed to drop out." Sahra, 16, sophomore.

3. "I would definitely need very good teachers. Teachers who care a lot, who remember what it's like to go through different teenage things. I'd have as many activities as I could possibly have to get the kids more interested. I'd try to get as many students as possible involved in the decision-making process, in the afterschool activities. I would definitely like to not have tests like CSAPs. I think that the SATs and ACTs are enough for them. They don't need to be stressed out about anything else. I'd have more advanced classes for students who are on that level. I would need some kind of intervention for kids that are being bullied." Erin, 18, senior.

4. "It would be a high school where there was no violence, no fighting. A high school where all teachers cared about their students and none of them let their students fall through the cracks. A high school where everyone was involved in activities—extracurriculars and sports. A school where you feel safe and you enjoy coming every day." Nichelle, 18, senior.

5. "They'd have to have a really good curriculum, something that fits each individual's needs, something that can help everyone, that is easy for everyone to adapt to. They'd have great teachers like our teachers now. You can actually get to know them. If you have a problem, you're not scared or intimidated. You can be open with everyone so you're actually able to learn." Elizabeth, 14, freshman.

6. "My ideal high school would be a place where the students' needs were always met. Instead of one teacher per classroom, you'd put two teachers per classroom so no one could get away with anything. There'd be a lot more funding so you could do more clubs and stuff. There would be security people that actually cared about the students instead of their jobs." Levi, 19, senior.

In another look at student motivation and what students in middle school think about themselves, their schools, and their peers, Daniels (2005) learned that they feel under a lot of stress and "crowded" with the social pressures of meeting new people, hormonal changes, and heavier homework load. They often feel they are the only ones experiencing stress or facing problems. Therefore, they feel it is helpful for teachers to talk about their own experiences in handling stress and what coping skills they have learned. Daniels concluded that the best ways to help students learn these skills is through their teachers modeling how to persevere and master stress and frustration.

Students are vocal in saying "good teachers care." They don't want easy teachers; they want those who care about student learning, hold high expectations, and provide the necessary supports for all students to succeed. They want teachers who use multiple assessments to determine learning needs and allow multiple paths to the same outcomes.

Figure 6.3   Learner-Centered Strategies for Creating Positive Relationships and a Positive Climate for Learning

To create a positive climate for learning, it is important to

- foster a caring personal relationship with each student,
- create caring personal relationships with their peers.

If teachers create a positive climate and relationships with their students, the students will feel cared about and that they belong.

> ### Demonstrate to my students that I appreciate each as an individual.

- Have private conferences with each student about how you could help make school a positive experience, and carry out what is agreed to as a way to establish a positive relationship and feelings of trust.
- Build on students' strengths by providing opportunities for them to take on traditional roles such as leaders, facilitators, and evaluators.
- Show respect for students' ideas and opinions, using phrases such as, "That's an interesting point. I hadn't thought of that before." or "You have a different perspective. Can you tell me more?"
- Show a personal interest in areas that are relevant to students (e.g., discuss their favorite sports, hobbies, jobs, job searches).

> ### Provide positive emotional support and encouragement to students who are insecure about performing well.

- Help students excel beyond their own expectations in ways that show an understanding of their learning and motivational needs (e.g., show students examples of what they have accomplished and what they can do to go beyond these accomplishments).
- Give students appropriate demonstrations that you care, such as showing concern in response to what they express as of concern to them, praising them for difficult accomplishments, and encouraging them when they are afraid they might fail.
- Praise students' efforts to accomplish learning tasks as well as growth in knowledge and skills.
- Provide safe environments for students to express their thoughts and opinions about what they are learning, such as small group settings or individual conferences.

> ### Demonstrate to students that I care about them as individuals.

- Communicate with students personally every day, and be responsive to information you have learned about their needs and concerns.
- Show understanding by identifying underlying feelings when students "act out" to show that you acknowledge and understand their feelings, e.g., "You seem frustrated and discouraged."
- Encourage parent involvement and shared responsibility for student learning by calling home often to communicate each learner's progress and needs, and to solicit parent input on needed support for their child(ren).
- Set up an area in your classroom that is always accessible to students for appropriate teacher or peer conversations.

(Continued)

Figure 6.3 (Continued)

| **Appreciate my students for who they are beyond whatever their accomplishments might be.** |

- Show you value students' ideas as worthy of discussion by allowing class time for discussion and follow-up on any new learning directions or topics, as appropriate, to validate students' ideas.

- Use "what if" situations with students to facilitate their development of personal responsibility for their own behaviors, e.g., "What if you talked to Aaron and tried to negotiate a compromise?"

- Express interest in students' personal lives, such as by asking them about their plans and goals or taking the time to discuss current events that impact their lives (e.g., youth crime and violence issues).

- Carefully listen to students' opinions and use what they express as a way to deepen your understanding of their thinking and feelings.

| **Help students value their abilities.** |

- Allow students to make choices whenever possible, such as choosing their own spelling lists or choosing their topic for a paper or project within a general subject area.

- When students encounter learning problems, encourage them to figure out their own solutions, providing assistance in problem-solving strategies as needed.

- Use peer tutoring or cross-age tutoring to provide opportunities for students to share their knowledge or demonstrate their skills with each other in pairs or small groups.

- Provide students with rubrics and content standards for all learning activities, and demonstrate high expectations combined with flexibility in ways students choose to demonstrate competence in these standards.

| **Help students feel like they belong in the class.** |

- Get to know student's background and personality so that this information can be used during class discussions as a way to respect student differences in their willingness to share opinions.

- Provide opportunities for students to practice social skills that help them feel socially comfortable, such as introducing each other to peers or adults, listening to each other's perspectives and providing feedback, interviewing classmates to find out their interests and hobbies, and assisting peers with academic or personal problems as appropriate.

- Pick a topic and have students brainstorm ideas; show similarities between students' ideas to demonstrate the similarities in ideas or thinking among students in the class.

- Arrange a special room where students can study or talk informally with each other without having to leave the building.

| **Treat students with respect.** |

- Provide a model of personal responsibility and integrity by such behaviors as keeping your promises to students and making only promises you know you can fulfill.

- Always keep appointments with students or, if changes in schedule are necessary, agree to mutually acceptable changes in appointment times.

- Help students establish and enforce classroom ground rules for personal interactions with the teacher and with each other.

- Confirm to your students that you believe they are capable of learning and achieving by making statements such as "I know you can solve that problem. It's like the one you solved last week. Give it a try and I'll check on how you are doing in a few minutes."

Regarding their peers, young adolescents want to feel part of a group and at the same time be unique. They say that their friends are those peers who "help me." They want to be able to share their worries and to have a support system. And they say they particularly need teachers who are willing to listen and really hear what they have to say.

Insights and Reflections: What Needs to Change in My Classroom?

As we studied learner-centered practices, we discovered many teachers who were highly learner centered. We met with them in focus groups and asked them to share with us what strategies they used that were most effective in each of the four major domains of classroom practice that we described earlier in this chapter. As you continue your journey to becoming learner centered in your classroom practices, it may be helpful for you to look at some of these strategies and ask yourself the degree to which you believe you implement these practices in your classrooms. We will focus on the first domain of Establishing Positive Relationships and a Positive Climate for Learning because it is universally important for students of all ages.

Look at the list of strategies our most learner-centered teachers say they use, shown in Figure 6.3. Rate how often you think you implement these practices. Then identify some changes you could make—perhaps in implementing

some version of some of these practices. Be sure to choose new practices that feel authentic to you, practices you are comfortable doing.

Finally, what insights have you had as you've been reading this chapter? As you reflect on your thoughts, insights, and questions, you will be preparing yourself for the next step in your journey: learning about tools that will help you become a learner-centered teacher.

What's Next?

In our final chapter, Chapter 7, we describe the tools you need in order to become learner centered. We begin the chapter by asking who's in charge of your learning and who's in charge of your students' learning. We include another mini-assessment for you to take so you can look again at your beliefs about learning, learners, and teaching; the instructional practices you use; how your students perceive your teaching; and how your peers perceive your teaching.

After you have taken the mini-assessment, you will have an opportunity to reassess the beliefs you hold about learners, learning, and teaching in light of what you learn from the mini-assessment and comparing your scores against the LCP rubric. We end the book by asking you to reflect on and consider your vision for schools as a way to begin planning to obtain the necessary resources for learner-centered schools and developing your own learner-centered classroom.

7

What Tools Do I Need to Become Learner Centered?

You've reached the point in this journey where you are ready for some more specific tools to help you become learner centered. We've seen that being learner centered is an individual thing that depends both on the characteristics of teachers and on the types of practices they implement. Moreover, we have also learned that teachers are not always the best judges of what is learner centered and what isn't. Rather, it is the perceptions of students as they experience teachers and classrooms that have helped us define "learner centered."

There are certain "non-negotiables" that students must perceive in order to see practices as learner centered. These consist of some core elements that they experience from being in your classroom:

- *Choice:* Opportunities to choose what they learn, and/or how and

when they learn it, and/or under what conditions. Students understand they may have limited choice about content, but they appreciate having choices about how they can learn it; the time frame in which they have to learn it; and whether they work individually, in groups, under headphones, sitting on the floor, or slumped at a table. They regard these processes as positive indicators that their teacher is taking them into account and valuing them as learners.

- *Responsibility:* Opportunities to take responsibility for their own learning. Students tell us they are much more motivated to learn when their teachers assume they (the students) are responsible for their learning. When teachers assume the responsibility for students' learning, students tell us they feel the learning they are expected to do has little if anything to do with them, their interests, or their learning needs.

- *Relevance:* Learning skills, processes, and information that are relevant to their lives. The relevance of what students are learning is closely related to their taking responsibility for their own learning. Students say they are more motivated to learn when their teachers take the time to learn what is relevant to them and to structure their classrooms around that relevance.

- *Challenge:* Learning that is challenging, yet not impossible. Students want to be challenged and appreciate teachers who can challenge them to perform at their highest levels while at the same time not intimidating them. Learner-centered teachers understand the importance of optimal challenge and how to provide this for each individual student. As one of our learner-centered teachers explained, it is important that students also learn to accept their own mistakes while challenging themselves. As this teacher put it, "I want my students to know that mistakes are great moments! One of my students showed he got the message as he told me, 'I just had a great moment; I got a B instead of the A I expected in science. Guess I need to focus more, huh?'"

- *Control:* Opportunities to control aspects of the learning environment, especially how the classroom functions. These functions include classroom rules for how students interact with each other and their teacher, how tardies and absences are handled, what to do about disruptive students, how to handle assignments turned in late, and how homework is assigned. Students report that when they have a say in classroom functioning, they feel engaged, treated fairly, and respected. Even more important, when students have a voice, they "own" the rules and classroom procedures, making the job of classroom management much easier for teachers.

- *Connection:* Experiences that contribute to students feeling connected to their peers, their teacher(s), their school, and their community. Just as students must feel connected to the content and perceive its relevance to their interests and lives, to achieve maximum learning and motivation to learn and stay in school, they must also feel positive social and emotional connections throughout their experiences of being in school. Students from elementary through high school report that teachers who get them involved in school governance, extracurricular school activities, and community service learning projects feel more a part of their school community and connected to their classmates and teachers.

- *Respect:* An atmosphere of mutual respect. Students say that the best teachers are those who both command and show respect for individual students and their diverse needs and backgrounds in their classrooms and teach students to appreciate that others have a right to their views—views that might be important to know. These teachers take individual learners and their learning seriously. They also model a respectful attitude toward others.

- *Competence:* Opportunities for each student to show competence. Students report that they learn better in classrooms in which the teacher builds activities and processes through which they can feel they are learning, can be successful learners in a variety of content areas, and feel that they are accomplishing something important. Learner-centered teachers know how to structure classroom activities so that students can be successful in mastering their own quality standards of achievement.

- *Cooperation:* An atmosphere of mutual cooperation and collaboration. Students say that the best teachers are those who model what it means to cooperate, that is, to be co-learners and collaborators in learning. These learner-centered teachers understand that competition may sometimes be helpful to introduce a spirit of fun into potentially boring classroom activities, but that competition can also give some students the message that they will not be as successful as other students. This can hamper these students' intrinsic motivation and their understanding of the value of cooperation as a strategy to achieve shared academic and social classroom goals.

- *Relationships:* Opportunities to build relationships with peers and teachers. Students say they learn better in classrooms in which they develop meaningful and positive relationships with their teacher and their classmates. They feel safe to make mistakes and not be ridiculed. They also learn to respect diverse perspectives and ways of teaching and learning. From students' perspectives, teacher practices that promote positive relationships are the most important contributors to motivating them to learn and do their best.

To know what your students are experiencing, you need a way to assess your views and compare them to your students' perceptions. Before we explore the tools for this assessment and comparison, let's first take a look at how you view your own learning.

Who's in Charge of My Learning?

Most of us teach the way we were taught, which means most of us do what we observed our teachers doing. However, if you carefully examine how you teach, does your teaching accurately reflect what you know and believe about learning? Remember the questions we asked you in Chapter 1 about how you solved the puzzle problem? One of our purposes in asking those questions was to help you recognize and articulate your preferred approaches and strategies for learning something new.

Another purpose was to illustrate the fact that you know how to go about your own learning, whether or not you are consciously aware of it. When we asked you to figure out the puzzle picture, you had a choice about whether to "play" the game, that is, to engage in learning how to approach a problem unlike others you have previously encountered. If you decided to play, you then activated various strategies you have used successfully with other problems that seem similar to this one. If you are one of the majority of people who have difficulty "solving" the puzzle, you couldn't figure it out using approaches you have used before, so you probably read further and discovered the strategies we supplied, one of which triggered recognition of what the puzzle depicts. The point is that you were the one making the decisions about how to proceed. You were in charge of your learning at all times. Even though we provided some hints and guidance, you made the decisions about what would work for you or whether you would even continue trying to learn how to solve the puzzle.

If you decided to engage in the process of learning the puzzle, how did you feel when you solved it? Take a few minutes to journal your responses to the following questions:

- Did you feel a sense of closure?
- Were you interested in the details of why the puzzle is difficult for most people?
- Did you share the puzzle with anyone else? If so, did you teach them how to solve it? Did you enjoy that teaching?
- Would you like to see how you'd do with another, similar puzzle now that you have learned how to solve the first one? If so, what would you do differently this time?

We have learned that the best teachers—those who inspire students to their highest learning potentials—understand not only how they and their students learn, but also the vast array of learning styles, preferences, and approaches they and their students use. These learner-centered teachers also understand the strategies that are most effective for teaching and learning. The comment in the box below captures much of this attitude.

A comment from a new high school teacher
(*Rocky Mountain News*, April 18, 2005)

In the beginning, I was the teacher I was trained to be. I was the open, holistic teacher whose classrooms should be completely democratic and let's let students make decisions and that sort of thing. . . . I kept saying, "Why aren't they learning? I'm doing everything I was taught to do! . . . I'm using a curriculum that the district paid millions for. I'm using these great books, letting them choose, letting them take control of their learning." I had to throw most of that out the window. I learned that a lot of students need security and stability first. Everything had to be structured, everything made explicit and expectations clear . . . and my students this semester have learned way more.

We've also learned that when teachers undertake the journey to learner-centered practices and policies, they set into motion a change strategy that people can't resist.

Here's why it's an irresistible change:

- The learner-centered model and process for change are built on both evidence-based data and intuitive knowledge. Together they form the impetus and direction needed to transform classrooms and schools into the types of learning environments that lead to optimal outcomes for all learners in the system.
- The change strategy provides a voice to all stakeholders—students, their families, teachers, administrators—regarding which goals should guide a reform in practices, how the reform should take place, who should be involved, and what the reform should look like during the change process. Everyone impacted by the change has a role and age-appropriate voice in setting the terms of direction and designing specific plans and procedures.
- The change processes match natural, organic individual and system functions and processes. This means that what we know to be the principles of learning and change provide the foundation for how the change is implemented. We know that people are naturally resistant to (and sometimes afraid of) change. We also know that people are naturally motivated to learn and that they learn continually, whether or not they are aware of it. Throughout the change process, these natural functions and processes are honored and respected. The people impacted by the change are encouraged to recognize their resistance and fear and reflect on how these feelings show up in themselves. They are also

encouraged to recognize their natural proclivities to learn and to reflect on how those proclivities manifest in themselves.

The change process, principles, and procedures all move in the direction of positive learning and change—away from negative emotions (fear) and toward positive emotions (love and altruism). When the people involved begin feeling overwhelmed or when anticipated changes aren't occurring as intended, the core values mutually defined by all stakeholders are the glue to keep things moving in the committed and intended direction.

Who's in Charge of Students' Learning?

Think back for a moment to Chapter 1 and the article by Jane Tompkins (1990) we suggested you read. In the article, Tompkins reflects on her shift from thinking she was in charge of her students' learning to thinking she was responsible for joining with them in learning. When teachers gain the understanding that all of us—teachers and their students alike—need a blend of teacher guidance, structure, support, and choice in learning new concepts and skills, some amazing learning outcomes are possible. The student outcomes we have validated in our research (McCombs, 2004b, 2005) include those shown in Figures 7.1 and 7.2.

To achieve these diverse outcomes, teachers incorporated the following core components into their practices:

1. Learner-centered teachers constructed learning activities that allowed students to be actively

Figure 7.1   Student Academic and Behavioral Outcomes Likely With Learner-Centered Practices

- High levels of classroom achievement on indicators such as grades and test scores
- High levels of classroom and school attendance and engagement
- High levels of social and emotional skills
- High levels of lifelong learning skills
- Low levels of disruptive classroom behaviors

Figure 7.2   Student Motivational Outcomes Likely With Learner-Centered Practices

- Take responsibility for their own learning
- Engage in learning for understanding vs. grades
- Achieve high academic and personal standards
- Engage in independent learning activities
- Seek out further information about topics of interest
- Persist in the face of learning challenges
- Continue to refine their skills in chosen areas
- Go beyond minimal assignments

engaged in creating their own knowledge and understanding. Examples include the following:

- Young children drew pictures or created plays to show they had mastered targeted reading and writing concepts and skills.
- Middle grade students picked questions that interested them, within and across content disciplines. Their teachers then arranged inquiry-based projects in keeping with state and national content standards.
- At the high school level, students organized service learning projects to better understand government and economic policies in a variety of social areas, or they took field trips to understand how scientists applied math and physics concepts in advanced science and technology careers.

2. Learner-centered teachers structured classroom procedures and learning activities to make sure that students' perspectives—interests, goals, needs, ways of thinking—were attended to and respected.

Examples include the following:

- Young children could select three ways to build an original story to share with their classmates, one of which had to be in words. The children selected the other two from a list that included singing the story as a song, acting out the story (with costumes and easy-to-assemble props), illustrating the story with drawings and/or paintings, arranging a choral reading with one or more classmates.

- Middle grade students selected social studies projects—to be presented to classmates—on the American Civil War from a list that included the following:

  o Prepare an oral journal telling the story of a slave who escapes through the Underground Railroad.
  o Design and make a board game showing the major battles of the war.
  o Write a military song for the Yankees and one for the Confederates.
  o Design and make a comic book telling the story of the war.
  o Prepare for and participate in a debate on the two sides of the war. First debate the Confederate position; then switch sides and debate the Yankee position.
  o Write a book report on *Behind Rebel Lines: The Incredible Story of Emma Edmonds, Civil War Spy.*
  o Design and illustrate five costumes worn by Emma Edmonds in the book *Behind Rebel Lines: The Incredible Story of Emma Edmonds, Civil War Spy.*
  o Design and illustrate a crossword puzzle using vocabulary from the Civil War.

- High school students in a science class were offered the following choices about how they wanted to approach learning about the human body:

  o Surviving extremes: how the human body copes with extreme heat and extreme cold.
  o Culture and obesity: perceptions, stereotypes, and health.
  o Human history: Where did we come from?
  o Human genomes and race: Are we alike or different?
  o Who is at risk for AIDS?
  o How the brain works and how it has evolved.
  o Eating disorders: food as an enemy.

- Once they had selected their topic, they specified their plan of action, using the following outline:

  o Determine and describe primary and secondary resources.
  o Determine format(s) for final project: written, oral, film, audio, Internet, other.
  o Determine intended audience for the project.
  o Gather and organize information.

o Prepare and turn in first draft of final project.
o Respond to teacher feedback; gather more information if needed; refine project.
o Prepare final project.
o Present final project to teacher, classmates, parents, others.
o Respond to feedback from audience.

3. Learner-centered teachers realized that students and teachers are partners in caring relationships, and they were willing to be co-learners and co-creators of learning experiences, including how technology is used to support learning. Examples of how these teachers participated as co-learners and co-creators of learning experiences include the following:

– One second-grade teacher and his students e-mailed friends and relatives, asking them to send examples of art from around the world as part of a unit on different nations. Once they had collected a sizable number of examples, the teacher guided the students in discussing common elements such as color, line, texture, composition, style (e.g., representational, nonrepresentational), themes and/or elements depicted (e.g., religious ideas, political themes) for use later in their own artwork that would be part of the finished project. Because he did not know ahead of time which nations would be represented in the collection, the teacher joined with his students in learning about them as they studied the collection. Together they compiled a notebook of facts about each nation, including

o Its history and length of time as a nation,
o Customs of the people/tribe or peoples/tribes,
o Primary religion(s),
o Governing body/bodies,
o Geography and economic situation (e.g., what it produces and exports; what it imports),
o General educational data,
o Indigenous foods,
o What it is most famous for,
o Examples of its art and artists.

In each section of the notebook, the teacher and students included examples of their own art that reflected what they had learned about that nation, how their learning had affected them as learners, and an idea they wished to convey about themselves and/or each particular nation.

– A typical learner-centered approach to joining middle school students as co-learners and incorporating technology into the learning experience is producing videos and Web sites to illustrate what is happening in the classroom. For instance, in a Web site about their classroom, an eighth-grade class and their teacher described their most recent experiences and projects, and included digital photos of art and science projects, scanned examples of writing (both narrative and expository), and short videos of a science project in which they built a computer from component parts. One video clip featured the teacher, who did not know how to build the computer beforehand, talking about how much she had learned about computers and about teamwork.

– One high school teacher in the Midwest devised a way to help her students increase their reading levels by capitalizing on their interest in restoring a tractor owned by one student's grandfather. Although the teacher knew nothing about restoring tractors, she knew that several students were adept mechanics—at least, with cars. To her surprise, the students decided to create two teams: a boys' team and a girls' team.

The class collected several tractor restoration manuals from the local library and located one manual for maintaining a John Deere Model B tractor at one student's aunt's home. Each team searched the Internet for information and discovered that there were regional and national tractor restoration competitions. They decided to pool resources and enter both teams in the regional competition, where they would be required to offer a polished presentation of their project, including an oral summary of the project, a workbook detailing the entire process (mechanical overhauls of the engine,

auxiliary and ancillary systems, and the external appearance of the tractor), and a business summary describing equipment maintenance, teamwork, project management, budgeting, planning, and marketing.

4. Learner-centered teachers made certain they knew each of their students personally and academically, and that students' individual differences (e.g., in learning rates, styles, talents, abilities) were adapted to, respected, and allowed to flourish.

– In the preceding example of the second-grade teacher and his students who began studying nations through their art, the teacher encouraged students to experiment with different media, styles, themes, and compositions, and to think of ways the same ideas could be expressed in other ways, for example, through music, performance, or writing. For each piece of art they produced, the teacher and students also produced an accompanying story, poem, song, outline for a short performance piece, or an oral or written explanation.

– In the preceding example of the middle school class constructing a Web site for their classroom, the teacher and students as a group decided on the content they wanted to include on the site, and included a short statement from each regarding what was learned during the project.

– Then the class broke into small groups to accomplish the following: overall design of the Web site and its navigation system; inserting content into the design (e.g., inserting content into an existing shell or writing some HTML code for links); video production (e.g., editing the audio and video taken during the project and assembling discrete audio and video files into the existing shell); technical management (e.g., uploading files, maintaining link integrity, responding to e-mail queries).

– The two teams of high school students engaged in tractor restoration each met with their teacher to discuss their learning strengths before undertaking the project. The team members, including the teacher, described their most likely contributions to the team, what they would like to learn from the project, and what they expected from the team. Each team then assigned specific roles to each person, periodically devoting a short meeting to evaluate how the team was proceeding and to plan any changes that needed to be made. Four times during the project (which extended over the school year), each team hosted the members' families for a show and tell in preparation for their presentation at the regional competition in the spring.

The bottom line and fundamental concept in being learner centered is something we have repeated often throughout this book: teachers need to truly understand from their own experience the importance of sharing power and control with learners. Understanding this truth means that teachers know that (a) we own what we create; (b) responsibility is based on having some choice and control; (c) learning, change, and achievement can't be mandated; and (d) without a sense of ownership, there is no responsibility; rather, there is blaming and compliance (or not!).

Implications for Practice

Understanding in a personal way the essence of learner-centered practices can help you see some important implications for your own practices, as well as those of other teachers in your school and district. Some of the implications we think are most important are the following.

Practice Implication #1: The educational context must support and value individual learners *and* learning outcomes. This means that an emphasis on standards and testing cannot take precedence over individual learners. In fact, our work shows that when the policies, procedures, and practices of a school or district focus on making certain that individual learners are acknowledged, appreciated, and supported, learner outcomes improve.

Practice Implication #2: Students must be active partners in co-creating caring and challenging classroom experiences, climate, and community. As we've said earlier, our work makes clear that engaging students as partners in the entire educational process results in fewer discipline problems, higher attendance rates, and improved student achievement.

Practice Implication #3: Teachers need adequate time and support to reflect on self and practices. This is actually a corollary of Practice Implication #1: The educational context must value individual learners (in this case, teachers) and learning outcomes (in this case, morale, teacher retention, days at work, and career longevity). When teachers work in a setting that honors them as learners, provides the resources for them to reflect on themselves and their practices, they are more likely to come to work rather than call in sick, stay rather than transfer to another school or district, make education a lifelong career, and enjoy a high morale that they are eager to share.

Practice Implication #4: Along with restructuring of policies, curricula, and systems, a change in attitude is required. The act of reading this book is an opportunity to examine your attitude toward your students and yourself as a teacher. Take a moment to reflect on your thoughts as you have been reading this book. Do you notice that your attitude towards your students has shifted in any way? Have you changed your mind in any way as you've been learning about what it means to be learner centered? If so, how? Do you have new ideas about the practices you use in your classroom?

Implications for Policy

In addition to the implications for classroom and school practices, we have also learned that being learner-centered carries some important policy implications. Thinking through these policy implications can help you see a potential leadership role for yourself—a role you can play in transforming your classroom and school in ways that will maximize desired student learning outcomes and desired teacher attitudes and behaviors.

Policy Implication #1: To become learner centered, schools and districts must place the responsibility for learning on learners and commit to reducing control over the learning process. In other words, policy decisions at the school and district levels need to begin with the recognition that each individual—students, teachers, and administrators—is in charge of her or his own learning. This means that policy decisions need to reflect the need for adults to help students develop these abilities:

- recognizing how they learn best;
- strategies for learning information, skills, and/or material that is difficult for them;
- reflecting on their own learning and thinking processes;
- accessing and utilizing resources in their learning;
- working individually and in teams to complete a project; and
- capitalizing on the diversity of their classmates and teachers to improve their own learning outcomes.

Policy Implication #2: Schools and districts wishing to become learner centered must give as much attention and planning to the personal as well as the technical and organizational domains of education as a living system. This means designing and implementing policies that reflect not just the technical and organizational needs of the school or district, but the personal, motivational, and interpersonal needs of students, teachers, administrators, and families. School or district policy making must include these constituencies in order to reflect what each deems important for students to want to be in school and to be motivated to learn skills, material, and information that is relevant to their lives. School-level policy making about student dress, for example, could begin with the formation of a team of students, administrators, and family members charged with drawing up a draft dress code for presentation to the school community. Once the draft has been circulated, the team would schedule discussion groups of students, teachers, administrators, and family members as a way to gather feedback to refine the policy and present it for adoption by the school community.

Policy Implication #3: Schools wishing to become learner centered must provide opportunities for all people—students, teachers, administrators, and family members—to be learners. That is, these groups of people need to be able to make decisions in a creative and collaborative way about how their work gets done. For instance, in one school we worked with, the language arts teacher and students in her classroom teamed as co-learners to decide how each individual in the team (including the teacher) could best approach learning how to plan, develop, and write a persuasive essay. The team began with a definition of a persuasive essay, a list of required characteristics, a rubric for

evaluating their developing abilities to write a persuasive essay, and a set of model essays to read. Using the definition and characteristics, the team brainstormed various approaches to producing a satisfactory persuasive essay. After each team member selected one or two approaches to try, the team adjourned for four days, during which the members read the model essays, selected a topic, and planned their essays. Just before their next meeting, each member posted a copy of the plan on the classroom computer blackboard. At their next meeting, the members described their progress using the rubric; challenges and obstacles they had encountered; and materials, events, or interactions that were particularly helpful. The team continued in this manner through a set of three drafts. The project culminated in the posting of their final essays, followed by a team meeting in which they provided feedback to each other and used the rubric to evaluate their own learning.

Policy Implication #4: Schools wishing to become learner centered need to plan carefully to create a culture in which people are free to share their basic beliefs and values, especially when there are diverse and divergent viewpoints. Margaret Wheatley has shown in her research (Wheatley, 1999a) that people hold opposing views because we live in a world of opposites. We learn the most from those whose opinions differ most from our own, if we can find the space and process for respectful dialogue. Schools that are becoming learner centered must develop policies that include planned, periodic opportunities for respectful dialogue when people hold opposing beliefs about how to achieve their learner-centered goals. Such policies must also provide structured processes for participants to agree on a common direction and process for planning and realizing learner-centered goals.

Policy Implication #5: In schools wishing to become learner centered, the stakeholders—students, their families, teachers, administrators—must be the ones who develop their own culture of learning and change. In other words, this culture of learning and change must arise from the stakeholders rather than be imposed from outside. Further, this culture must support learner reflection, continuous examination, and improvement. The example we described in Policy Implication #3 above serves well here, too, as it shows how the stakeholders, the language arts teacher and her students, developed a team approach of learner reflection, examination of learning and skill, and continuing improvement over time. The process this team used offered multiple opportunities for its members to think about what they were learning, try out ways to develop a new skill, and solicit feedback from fellow members as a means for improving steadily over a matter of a few weeks.

Policy Implication #6: Policy development in schools wishing to become learner centered must be grounded in dialogue that includes all the stakeholders: students, teachers, families, administrators. Moreover, the processes of learning and change need to emerge from this inclusive dialogue, as exemplified by the language arts teacher and her students learning how to write a powerful persuasive essay. Through their formation of a learning team, these people used their relationships with each other and their ability to collaborate as the vehicle for changing from a "traditional" approach to learning how to write a persuasive essay to one that was learner centered, and, thus, more likely to produce the results each individual hoped for.

The Learner-Centered Surveys

Now you are ready to take the next step in your journey. This step takes courage and commitment. In this step, we ask you to learn information about, as well as experience the value of, self-assessment tools designed to help you reflect and think critically about your beliefs and practices. You had a preview of the process when you took the Teacher Beliefs Survey in Activity 2.1 in Chapter 2 and compared your scores on the mini-survey to the scores of teachers considered learner centered.

The tools we offer in this chapter offer you an opportunity for a more extensive and comprehensive examination of your educational theories and practices in the context of your beliefs and teaching experiences. The overall model that we have fine-tuned and validated in our 12-year research program is described in Figure 7.3.

Characteristics of Learner-Centered Tools

The assessment models and tools used in most schools and districts to show that teachers are "qualified" and meet quality teaching standards are

Figure 7.3   The Learner-Centered Model

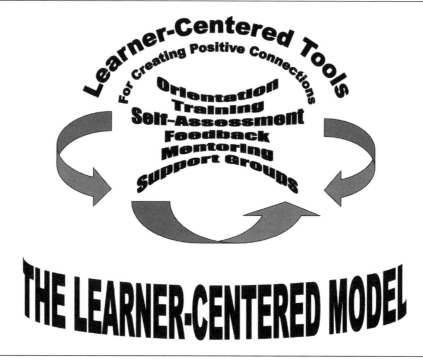

typically dreaded by most teachers and their superiors. Teacher evaluations are usually conducted by the administrators in the building and involve the administrator visiting the teachers' classrooms at an unannounced time to observe/rate what they do or don't do during a single class or class period. Teachers are on their "best behavior" but inwardly quaking in fear that their principal or other administrator will somehow not see all the great things that have gone into preparing that lesson. Sound familiar?

When we observed what usually happened during teacher evaluations and saw that they led to very few constructive outcomes or changes in practice that were welcomed by teachers, we knew something else was needed. The self-assessment and reflection model we developed is one defined by assessments that *are*

- nonthreatening,
- tools for learning and change,
- opportunities to share expertise,

and are not

- evaluations of competence,
- one-size-fits-all strategies,
- "cookbook" teaching procedures.

In other words, what we have created is a set of tools for teachers and their students that *can make the process of change a process of learning.* We have seen how these tools can reinvigorate teachers and students alike and help bring back the joy of teaching and learning.

The Assessment of Learner-Centered Practices (ALCP): Tools for Creating Learner-Centered Classrooms and Departments

We have developed and validated four slightly different versions of our ALCP self-assessment and reflection tools for students and teachers:

1. Grades K–3,

2. Grades 4–8,

3. Grades 9–12, and

4. college levels.

Though each version differs slightly across schooling levels, they all include two sets of surveys, one for the instructor and one for students. The instructor surveys provide teachers with an opportunity to increase their awareness of their impact on students by assessing three areas:

1. instructor beliefs and assumptions about learners, learning, and teaching;

2. instructor characteristics related to effective teaching; and

3. instructor assessment of classroom practices in areas most related to student motivation and achievement.

The student surveys identify students not being reached through

- student assessment of classroom practices (the same areas as on the instructor assessments); and

- student assessments of motivation in seven areas shown by the research to be most related to a variety of positive academic and social outcomes.

The specific variables measured in each survey for the Grades 4–8 levels of schooling are shown in Figure 7.4. Explanations or sample items are shown for each of the teacher and student variables, along with the rubric generated from validation samples.

As you can see, there is considerable useful information that teachers and students can use to see how close they are to the research-validated "Learner-Centered Rubric" (LCR). The LCR gives teachers and students a way to compare their individual and class scores to samples from teachers who had the most highly motivated and highest achieving students in the United States. To evaluate your individual scores relative to the LCR, the main things to look for are (1) Do your scores more closely align with the LCR this time compared with the first time you took the survey in Chapter 2? (2) Are there specific areas where you notice that your thinking has changed as a result of reading up to this point?

When teachers and students in your school—and when you, yourself—take the complete teacher and student ALCP surveys, you will have an opportunity to participate in a guided reflection process (explained below) to identify scores that are above and below the LCR, identify for yourself areas that could benefit from change, and make a personal self-development plan to get the mentoring and support you need to make the changes you desire.

Figure 7.4   Variables Measured in the Assessment of Learner-Centered Practices (ALCP) Surveys

Teacher Variables	Explanation (Definition or Example)	Grades 4–8 LC Rubric**
Teacher Beliefs		
Learner-centered beliefs about learners, learning, & teaching.	I believe that just listening to students in a caring way helps them solve their own problems.	High ≥ 3.2
Non-learner-centered beliefs about learners	There are some students whose personal lives are so dysfunctional that they simply do not have the capability to learn.	Low ≤ 2.4
Non-learner-centered beliefs about learning and teaching	I can't allow myself to make mistakes with my students.	Low ≤ 2.7
Teacher Perceptions of Classroom Practices		
Creates positive interpersonal relationships/climate	I demonstrate to each student that I like him/her as an individual.	High ≥ 3.5
Honors student voice, provides individual learning challenges	I encourage students to express their own unique thoughts and beliefs.	High ≥ 3.5
Encourages higher order thinking and self-regulation	I teach children a variety of learning strategies.	High ≥ 3.3
Adapts to individual developmental differences	I get to know each student's unique background.	High ≥ 3.0
Teacher Self-Efficacy	Beliefs in competency to be an effective teacher and facilitator of learning for all students.	High ≥ 3.0
Reflective Self-Awareness	Degree to which teacher is aware of the influence of thoughts and feelings on actions and tends to analyze and reflect on personal or professional experience	High ≥ 3.0
Autonomy Support	Degree to which teacher believes learning is best supported by:	
Moderately Controlling	Moderate teacher control and direction of learning.	High ≥ 3.2
Highly Controlling	High teacher control and direction of learning.	Low ≤ 3.1
Moderately Autonomy Supportive	Moderate level of support for student choice and personal control over learning.	Low ≤ 2.6
Highly Autonomy Supportive	High level of support for student choice and personal control over learning.	High ≥ 3.0
Student Perceptions of Classroom Practices		
Creates positive interpersonal relationships/climate	My teacher likes me.	High ≥ 3.1

Student Variables	Explanation (Definition or Example)	LC Rubric
Honors student voice, provides individual learning challenges	My teacher listens carefully to what I am saying.	High ≥ 2.9
Encourages higher order thinking and self-regulation	My teacher helps me remember what I learn.	High ≥ 3.1
Adapts to individual developmental differences	My teacher asks me what I do when I'm not in school.	High ≥ 2.8
Differences Between Student and Teacher		
Perceptions of Classroom Practices		Low ≥ 0 to −.6
Creates positive interpersonal relationships/climate	Student's ratings of teacher's positive relationships minus teacher's rating.	Low ≥ −.3
Honors student voice, provides individual learning challenges	Student's ratings of teacher's honoring student voice minus teacher's rating.	Low ≥ −.6
Encourages higher order thinking and self-regulation	Student's ratings of teacher's encouraging higher order thinking minus teacher's rating.	Low ≥ 0.3
Adapts to individual developmental differences	Student's ratings of teacher's adaptation to individual differences minus teacher's rating.	Low ≥ −.6
Student Learning and Motivation Variables		
Self-Efficacy	Beliefs in competency to learn and achieve.	High ≥ 3.5
State Epistemic Curiosity	Knowledge-seeking curiosity in learning.	High ≥ 3.1
Active Learning Strategies	Strategies directed at being actively engaged while learning.	High ≥ 3.1
Effort Avoidance Strategies	Strategies directed at avoiding effort while learning.	Low ≤ 1.9
Task Mastery Goals	Intrinsic motivational orientation directed to learning and mastering task goals.	High ≥ 3.4
Performance Oriented Goals	Extrinsic motivational orientation to achieve high grades or scores rather than learn.	Low ≤ 2.7
Work Avoidance Goals	Motivational orientation to avoid assignments and other work involved in learning.	Low ≤ 2.1
Achievement Scores	Teacher-assigned classroom achievement score on a scale from 0 to 100.	High ≥ 90.3

NOTES: All variables have scores ranging from 1 to 4 except Achievement Scores, which range from 0 to 100.

**Learner-Centered Rubric based on scores from classrooms in prior validation sample (Weinberger & McCombs, 2003) that had the highest student achievement and motivation.

The most important point for us—and we hope for you as well—is that the ALCP surveys can be used to facilitate your (and your colleagues') journey to learner-centered practices. Our validation research has confirmed that to reach the needs of all learners in your classrooms and schools, all faculty and teaching styles are needed. Even the most learner-centered teachers do not reach all students, and even the least learner-centered teachers reach some students. All faculty/teachers are needed in a system if all students are to be reached. Furthermore, no single teaching style, learning program, or instructional strategy is best for all students and teachers. The good news is that being "learner centered" truly means discovering, designing, and implementing the best approaches for each diverse teacher and learner.

A second major finding from our research is that there are no single best effective strategies and effective teaching practices for all content areas and learning standards/skills to be acquired. Our research demonstrated that there is a range of effective teaching practices for different kinds of learning and disciplines. Finally, our research helped reveal that for individuals and the system to successfully change to become more learner centered, a process was needed for expertise to be recognized and successful strategies to be shared. We confirmed the research findings of others (e.g., Fullan, 2001) that the best experts are already in a system. What is needed are group- and community-building processes to bring their expertise to the surface and facilitate the sharing of successful strategies and approaches.

Research-Validated Definition of "Learner Centered"

Our research over the past 12 years has shown us what it means to be learner centered from a research or evidence-based perspective (McCombs, 2004b, 2005). We weren't exactly sure what we would find from the research, but we did know that results would greatly extend what is currently known about what defines "best practices" from the perspective of both teachers and their students. At a general level, being learner centered (a) is a reflection of the LCPs in the programs, technologies, practices, policies, and people that support learning for all learners in the system; (b) balances the concern with learning and achievement and the concern with diverse learner needs; (c) is a complex interaction of qualities of the technology in combination with characteristics of instructional practices, as perceived by individual learners; and (d) meaningfully predicts learner motivation and levels of learning and achievement.

In summary, what we have learned is that when teachers are being learner centered, their practices won't look the same from day to day, class to class, department to department. Learner-centered teachers understand that they must remain flexible and constantly in tune with and adapting to students' changing learning needs. Learner-centered teachers also understand that "learner centered" is in "the eye of the beholder": what one student needs and perceives will not be the same as another student in the same class. When teachers can learn to act on student perceptions and not worry whether these are "right or wrong" from their perspective, they have taken a huge step toward being learner centered. Finally, learner-centered teachers know that "learner centeredness" depends on the needs of individual learners, the culture of the school and district, and characteristics of the surrounding community. What works in other school systems or even other content areas in the same system may not necessarily work with this student and this class.

ALCP Feedback Process for Teachers

How do teachers learn from the ALCP survey experience? As we worked out how best to share what teachers could learn from the ALCP teacher and student surveys they had administered to a class of students and/or across a school building or district, we wanted to develop an effective process for individual and group ALCP feedback. The process we designed, tested, and validated is called the Guided Reflection and Feedback Process. Through this process, we offer support and guidance for teachers by providing

- individual and confidential feedback on scores relative to the Learner-Centered Rubric;
- time for reflection on areas of beliefs or practices that could shift in more learner-centered directions; and
- encouragement for faculty to take personal responsibility for ongoing learning and continuous improvement of practice.

The main purpose of the guided reflection process is to help teachers feel comfortable with and excited about the changes they can make to enhance student learning and motivation. Using the ACLP surveys and going through the guided reflection process provide teachers with answers to these questions:

- How can I improve instruction and student achievement?
- How can I create a learner-centered environment?
- In which areas am I strong or weak when creating a learner-centered classroom?
- How can I best relate to my students both academically and interpersonally?
- In which areas can I accomplish my greatest professional development and growth?
- How can I use self-assessment as a tool for systemwide reform and change in thinking?

To see how the Guided Reflection and Feedback Process works and why it is particularly effective, we'll show you how to interpret some sample ALCP teacher feedback. Look at the example for a middle school teacher shown in Figures 7.5 and 7.6. Figure 7.5 shows the explanation the teacher in this example receives about the teacher and student variables that are measured and how these variables relate to desired student learning outcomes. Figure 7.5 also shows the teacher's individual scores on each of the teacher variables and how these scores compare to the desired score shown in the LC Rubric.

Figure 7.5 Assessment of Learner-Centered Practices (ALCP) Example Middle School Grade 7

Teacher Measures	Explanation (Definition of Example)	Your Score[1]	Grades 4–8 LC Rubric[2]
Teacher Beliefs			
Learner-centered beliefs about learners, learning, & teaching	I believe that just listening to students in a caring way helps them solve their own problems.	3.21	High ≥ 3.2
Non-learner-centered beliefs about learners	There are some students whose personal lives are so dysfunctional that they simply do not have the capability to learn.	2.11	Low ≤ 2.2
Non-learner-centered beliefs about learning and teaching	I can't allow myself to make mistakes with my students.	2.25	Low ≤ 2.5
Teacher Classroom Practices			
Creates positive interpersonal relationships/climate	I demonstrate to each student that I like him/her as an individual.	2.50	High ≥ 3.6
Honors student voice, provides challenge, and encourages perspective taking	I encourage students to express their own unique thoughts and beliefs.	2.50	High ≥ 3.5
Encourages higher order thinking and self-regulation	I teach children a variety of learning strategies.	2.50	High ≥ 3.4
Adapts to individual developmental differences	I get to know each student's unique background.	2.00	High ≥ 3.0
Teacher Self-Efficacy	Beliefs in competency to be an effective teacher and facilitator of learning for all students.	2.50	High ≥ 3.1
Teacher Beliefs About Middle Childhood	Beliefs that the teacher:		
Teachers can influence student learning during middle childhood.	Can influence student learning during middle childhood.	3.25	Higher ≥ 3.4
Difficult stage	Cannot have much impact on student learning during the difficult period of middle childhood.	3.00	Lower ≤ 2.8
Reflective Self-Awareness	Degree to which teacher is aware of the influence of thoughts and feelings on actions and tends to analyze and reflect on personal or professional experience.	3.20	High ≥ 3.0
Autonomy Support	Degree to which teacher believes learning is best supported by:		
Moderately Controlling	Moderate teacher control and direction of learning.	2.60	High ≥ 2.8
Highly Controlling	High teacher control and direction of learning.	3.40	Low ≤ 2.4
Moderately Autonomy Supportive	Moderate level of support for student choice and personal control over learning.	3.00	High ≥ 3.3
Highly Autonomy Supportive	High level of support for student choice and personal control over learning.	2.80	Low ≤ 2.9

SOURCE: *ALCP 4–8 Teacher Data February, 2003*

NOTES:

[1] Scores range from 1 to 4.

[2] LC Rubric is based on the scores of the 93 validation sample teachers with the highest proportion of students high in both achievement and motivation. For the validation sample, data were collected from 199 middle school teachers and 3,562 middle school students from nine states: TX, WA, MA, IL, ND, NJ, DC, PA, MI.

Understanding Sample ALCP Feedback: Table of Teacher Variables Compared to the Learner-Centered Rubric for One Teacher

The next part of the Guided Reflection and Feedback Process involves the teacher seeing how her or his students responded as a class. Figure 7.6 shows a sample teacher's students' perceptions of how frequently they experience each domain of learner-centered practice. The table then shows the discrepancy between the students' views of the frequency of learner-centered practices in the classroom and the teacher's view. Student self-assessments of their level of motivation in this teacher's class are also shown so that they can be compared with the rubric.

Now look at Figure 7.7, which shows a graph of the frequency of learner-centered practice each student in the teacher's classroom reported for each of the four domains of practice. In these four charts and the chart showing the discrepancy between the teacher and student perceptions of the frequency of learner-centered practices in each of the four domains, there is a graphic view of how each student experiences these practices in this teacher's classroom. During the guided reflection process, the teacher is helped to explore in what specific area of practice and for which students more learner-centered practices are needed. Although students are not identified, teachers generally know those they are reaching and those they are having trouble reaching. Seeing a visual representation provides the opportunity to focus in on particular practices and students. For the teacher shown in this example, attention during the guided reflection process begins with the first domain of practice, Creates Positive Interpersonal Relationships. The teacher is doing a moderately good job reaching about a third of the students (black bars on the graph), another third are saying the teacher only "sometimes" does these practices (e.g., demonstrating that she cares, treating the student with respect, helping the student feel like she or he belongs), and a final third are saying between "sometimes and almost never" the teacher does these practices for them. What we've learned is that when teachers begin to focus on the students who need extra attention and support, they improve things for the whole class. Beginning with the first domain of LC practices is also critical for improving student perceptions in the other three domains of practice.

For the teacher in the examples shown in Figures 7.5, 7.6, and 7.7, the guided reflection process gave her information she used to identify aspects of her beliefs and practices that could benefit from change. In the guided reflection, she was asked to express what the data meant to her and to identify possible areas of change in her beliefs and practices that could modify desired student outcomes for the better. She was given suggestions of strategies that have been successful for other teachers at her grade level and in the domains of practice in which she wanted to improve. Throughout the process, we remained mindful of our primary purpose: making certain the teacher remained comfortable with the idea of changing some of her beliefs and practices, while at the same time supporting her excitement in planning how she could enhance her students' motivation and learning.

Figure 7.6 Assessment of Learner-Centered Practices (ALCP) Example Middle School Grade 7

Student Measures	Explanation (Definition of Example)	Your Mean[1]	Score SD[2]	4–8 LC Rubric[3] Mean
Student Perception of Classroom Practices				
Creates positive interpersonal relationships/climate	My teacher likes me.	2.14	0.68	High ≥ 3.1
Honors student voice, provides challenge, and encourages perspective taking	My teacher listens carefully to what I am saying.	2.22	0.58	High ≥ 3.0
Encourages higher order thinking and self-regulation	My teacher helps me remember what I learn.	2.57	0.59	High ≥ 3.2
Adapts to individual developmental differences	My teacher asks me what I do when I'm not in school.	2.17	0.49	High ≥ 2.8
Differences Between Student and Teacher				Low ≤ 0 to –.2
Perception of Classroom Practices				or
Creates positive interpersonal relationships/climate	Student's ratings of teacher's positive relationships minus teacher's rating.	–0.36		Low ≤ –2
Honors student voice, provides challenge, and encourages perspective taking	Student's ratings of teacher's honoring student voice minus teacher's rating.	–0.28		Low ≤ –2
Encourages higher order thinking and self-regulation	Student's ratings of teacher's encouragement of higher order thinking minus teacher's rating.	0.07		Low ≤ 0
Adapts to individual developmental differences	Student's ratings of teacher's adaptation to individual differences minus teacher's rating.	0.17		Low ≤ –1
Student Learning and Motivation Variables				
Self-Efficacy	Beliefs in competency to learn and achieve.	2.72	0.79	High ≥ 3.6
State Epistemic Curiosity	Knowledge-seeking curiosity in learning.	2.27	0.75	High ≥ 3.1

Student Measures	Explanation (Definition of Example)	Your Mean[1]	Score SD[2]	4–8 LC Rubric[3] Mean
Active Learning Strategies	Strategies directed at being actively engaged while learning.	2.64	0.55	High ≥ 3.1
Effort Avoidance Strategies	Strategies directed at avoiding effort while learning.	2.05	0.94	Low ≤ 1.8
Task Mastery Goals	Intrinsic motivational orientation directed to learning and mastering task goals.	2.46	0.80	High ≥ 3.4
Performance Oriented Goals	Extrinsic motivational orientation directed to achieving high grades or scores rather than learning.	2.18	0.58	Low ≤ 2.6
Work Avoidance Goals	Motivational orientation directed to avoiding assignments and other work involved in learning.	2.27	0.60	Low ≤ 2.0
Achievement scores	Teacher-assigned classroom achievement score on a scale from 0 to 100.	73.16	23.65	High ≥ 90.4

SOURCE: *ALCP 4-8 Teacher Data February, 2003*

NOTES:
[1] Scores range from 1 to 4 except for achievement scores that range from 0 to 100.

[2] SD = Standard Deviation, the statistic that reflects the average difference among scores.

[3] LC Rubric is based on the scores of the 73 validation sample teachers with the highest proportion of students high in both achievement and motivation. For the validation sample, data were collected from 182 middle school teachers and 3,188 middle school students from nine states: TX, WA, MA, IL, ND, NJ, DC, PA, MI.

Figure 7.7   Mean Differences Between Student and Teacher Perceptions of Classroom Practices Teacher EXAMPLE

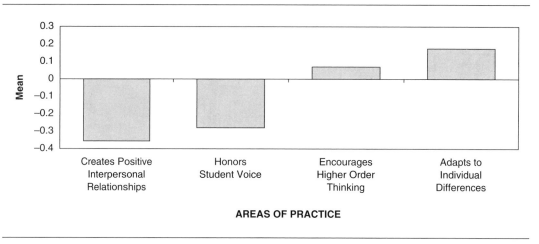

NOTE: Zero means that student and teacher perceptions are the same.

Time for another pause to stop, take a breath, and reflect on what you have been reading and thinking about up to this point. Take a moment to look at each of the following questions. Then give yourself time to write your responses to each in your journal.

1. What do I believe about learners, learning, and teaching?

2. What are my instructional practices in the classroom?

3. How do my students perceive my instructional practices?

4. How do my teaching peers perceive my instructional practices?

Becoming a Magnet for Change in My School and District

In working over the past decade with a variety of schools and districts in the United States and the United Kingdom, we have observed individual teachers playing a prominent leadership role in transforming their schools and districts. One of the ways this occurs is when teachers are willing to share their results with other teachers in their building or district. They take the risk of sharing what they learned about themselves and what their students reported about their practices. They do this so that others can see that the ALCP survey process not only benefits them individually, but the process is a way to share expertise and extend the probability of their colleagues using the most effective learner-centered practices.

One of the most effective ways that individual teachers and the school leadership team can extend the benefits of learner-centered practices and the use of the ALCP survey tools to other interested faculty is to understand how to use the LCM process for sharing group feedback:

• Determine a categorization system for the data (e.g., by department) that will protect individual faculty identities. The most useful categories to use are those that provide information to answer basic questions about differences in student learning and/or motivation that are occurring in different discipline areas, in different departments, or with different types of teachers (e.g., male versus female, experienced versus new teachers). Whatever categories are decided upon, the critical ingredient for promoting trust and protecting individual teacher identities is that the category include data from no fewer than three teachers.

- Schedule a meeting of all participants and department chairs or team leaders (as appropriate) to present the survey results and explain how to interpret these results using the LCR and LCM.

Because this meeting may be the first opportunity for some of the participants to learn details about the LCM and the LCR, it should be carefully planned and conducted. The person(s) conducting the meeting need to include these main points as they present the results and explain how to interpret them:

- The LCM is the product of years of research and reflects what the research evidence shows to be the best instructional practices.
- This body of research shows that teachers using learner-centered practices are much more likely to have students who are motivated to learn, like coming to these classrooms, and want to improve their achievement.
- The LCR reflects statistical data assembled from thousands of teachers using learner-centered instructional practices.

- Comparing one's own score with the LCR is a way to identify those practices that could benefit from change.
- Facilitating small group breakouts (e.g., by department or team) is a way to share faculty strengths and facilitate the change process. These breakout sessions help faculty plan how to (a) share the results more broadly throughout the school and/or district and (b) identify changes that will move the school and/or district toward more learner-centered practices. The small group breakouts should be designed to help faculty share their results in trustworthy and safe settings. Teachers should feel free to share their most successful areas of practice as well as areas in which they need support to improve. This step, sharing results with colleagues and working together to plan for desired changes, is a prerequisite for establishing learner-centered support groups that can model effective practices and mentor colleagues, which builds the school's capacity to continue its learner-centered journey.
- Following one or more meetings of the small groups, the next step is to identify the professional development needs both within and across groups. Deciding how to proceed in identifying these needs can occur at several levels. Because of this, the decision about how to proceed is unique to each group (school, district, region). In some instances, the decision is made by participating teachers; in other situations, departments, schools, or even districts make the decision. The box on the next page contains some

of the strategies we have observed for identifying professional

development needs based on the
LCM and the ALCP surveys.

Strategies for Determining Professional Development
Needs Based on the LCM and the ALCP

- Department or School Level

Identifying common areas of discrepancy from the ALCP Beliefs and Attitudes Surveys and the ALCP Instructor Characteristics Surveys for different kinds of courses and content areas. One way this strategy has been used is for the members of different departments or teams to identify their areas of biggest discrepancy and then to compare their results with other departments or teams to see which areas overlap. Those with the biggest overlap are identified as the areas to be addressed first in professional development programs. A second way this strategy has been used is for one person to look at the survey results for an entire building and identify the areas of largest discrepancy.

Identifying common areas of discrepancy from the ALCP Surveys for specific domains of practice. An individual or group can systematically examine the completed surveys across the four domains and identify the most common areas of discrepancy within each domain:

cognitive and metacognitive,
motivational and affective,
social and developmental, and
individual differences.

Identifying types of training and content needed. Once the areas of discrepancy have been identified, an individual or group can identify the resources available to provide specific types of training (e.g., demonstration teaching by LC teachers; focus groups of students providing feedback regarding classroom instructional practices, classroom climate, etc.; guided learning of new practices) and specific content.

- Classroom Level

Identifying common areas of discrepancy in domains of practice from the ALCP Classroom Practices Surveys (both the instructor surveys and the student surveys). Individual teachers compare their survey results to determine which practices are most discrepant from the LC rubric. In a process similar to that used at the school level, teachers agree to some common areas where all could benefit from further training, field trips to other model schools, or self-studies in certain areas where a number of teachers are struggling to identify new practices to reach their students.

Identifying common areas below desired rubric for teacher beliefs and other characteristics. Again, as teachers share their individual results with each other, some shared areas where teachers could work on particular beliefs and/or other characteristics will surface. Examples include having high scores on nonlearner-centered beliefs about learners (e.g., agreeing strongly with items such as "It's just too late to reach some students" or "Some students' personal lives are so dysfunctional they do not have the capability to learn"), having lower than ideal teacher self-efficacy, being lower in reflective self-awareness than ideal, or holding more controlling beliefs rather than autonomy supportive beliefs.

Identifying types of training and content needed. Once teachers identify common areas of practices, beliefs, or other characteristics as a group, they can discuss what types of training or other options they would like to engage in to become more learner-centered. These discussions should be structured so that everyone involved works together in order to identify and include options that all teachers in the group feel comfortable about.

Reassessing My Beliefs

Now it is time for you to take a look at your own progress during the journey we have been on in this book. Remember the short Teacher Beliefs Survey you did in Chapter 1? Here is another version of that survey, with some slightly different items, for you to use to assess any shifts you may have made.

After you have taken the second Teacher Beliefs Survey in Activity 7.1, compare your scores on the three scales with the rubric scores for each (in parentheses):

1. Learner-Centered Beliefs About Learners, Learning, and Teaching (3.2)

2. Non-Learner-Centered Beliefs About Learners (2.3)

3. Non-Learner-Centered Beliefs About Learning and Teaching (2.4)

Take a moment to consider your scores on the two surveys and record your reflections in your journal. Have your scores changed since the first time you took the survey in Chapter 2? If so, how have they changed? Are you surprised? If not, why not? If so, why do you think you are surprised? To what do you attribute the change(s)?

If your scores have not changed appreciably, why do you think they have remained constant? Again, are you surprised? To what do you attribute your unchanged score(s)?

What Is My Vision for Schools?

Reflecting on your beliefs about learners, learning, and instructional practices has most likely tapped into some ideas you have regarding schools and how they work. Have you taken time recently to articulate your vision for schools and all their myriad learners? Whether you have or have not, take a moment right now to think about what you believe would be the characteristics of the best schools. Write your thoughts in your journal before you read further.

We have done considerable thinking about schools and what we hope they will entail. One part of our vision for schools is that they produce lifelong learners. We know from our research that the more learner-centered schools and classrooms are, the greater the likelihood that students will develop the seven dimensions of "Learning Power" that our colleague, Ruth Deakin Crick, in Bristol, England, has found to define lifelong learners. Crick has identified seven dimensions of learning power, described as a set of continua of opposites. The box on page 133 shows these continua.

As you look over the seven dimensions of learning power that define the

(Text continues on page 133)

ACTIVITY 7.1(I)

The Assessment of Learner-Centered Practices (ALCP)
Teacher Beliefs Survey 1 (Short Form)©

Directions: Please read each of the statements below. Decide to what extent you agree or disagree with each statement. Circle the letter that best matches your choice for each statement. Go with your first judgment and do not spend too much time on any one statement. PLEASE ANSWER EVERY QUESTION.

A = Strongly Disagree • B = Somewhat Disagree • C = Somewhat Agree • D = Strongly Agree

		Strongly Disagree	Somewhat Disagree	Somewhat Agree	Strongly Agree
1.	In order to maximize learning, I need to help students feel comfortable in discussing their feelings and beliefs.	A	B	C	D
2.	It's impossible to work with students who refuse to learn.	A	B	C	D
3.	No matter how badly a teacher feels, s/he has a responsibility to not let students know about those feelings.	A	B	C	D
4.	Taking the time to create caring relationships with my students is the most important element for student achievement.	A	B	C	D
5.	I can't help feeling upset and inadequate when dealing with difficult students.	A	B	C	D
6.	If I don't prompt and provide direction for student questions, they won't get the right answer.	A	B	C	D
7.	I can help students who are uninterested in learning get in touch with their natural motivation to learn.	A	B	C	D
8.	No matter what I do or how hard I try, there are some students who are unreachable.	A	B	C	D
9.	Knowledge of the subject area is the most important part of being an effective teacher.	A	B	C	D

		Strongly Disagree	Somewhat Disagree	Somewhat Agree	Strongly Agree
10.	Students will be more motivated to learn if teachers get to know them at a personal level.	A	B	C	D
11.	Innate ability is fairly fixed, and some children just can't learn as well as others.	A	B	C	D
12.	One of the most important things I can teach students is how to follow rules and to do what is expected of them in the classroom.	A	B	C	D
13.	Being willing to share who I am as a person with my students facilitates learning more than being an authority figure.	A	B	C	D
14.	Even with feedback, some students just can't figure out their mistakes.	A	B	C	D
15.	I am responsible for what my students learn and how they learn.	A	B	C	D

ACTIVITY 7.1(II)

Scoring

A responses = 1 point   B responses = 2 points   C responses = 3 points   D responses = 4 points

Add your scores from items 1, 4, 7, 10, & 13   Total _____   Divide by 5 _____

Add your scores from items 2, 5, 8, 11, & 14   Total _____   Divide by 5 _____

Add your scores from items 3, 6, 9, 12, & 15   Total _____   Divide by 5 _____

Turn to page 133 to see how your scores compare with the learner-centered beliefs associated with the Learning-Centered Principles.

Interpretation Assessment of Learner-Centered Practices (ALCP) Teacher Beliefs Survey (Short Form)©

The Teacher Beliefs Survey Short Form has 15 of the 35 items that are on the long form. These 15 items comprise three subscales with 5 items on each scale. When you scored your responses on the Teacher Beliefs Survey Short Form, you added the total of your scores for each of the three subtests and divided by 5 to arrive at your average score for each subscale.

To get an idea of how your beliefs compare with what is considered learner centered, compare your scores on the three subscales with the rubric provided below.

Scale 1   Learner-Centered Beliefs about Learners, Learning, and Teaching

Items 1, 4, 7, 10, 13   My Score _____ (total ÷ 5)   Rubric Score ____3.2____

Scale 2   Non Learner-Centered Beliefs about Learners

Items 2, 5, 8, 11, 14   My Score _____ (total ÷ 5)   Rubric Score ____2.3____

Scale 3   Non Learner-Centered Beliefs about Learning and Teaching

Items 3, 6, 9, 12, 15   My Score _____ (total ÷ 5)   Rubric Score ____2.4____

SOURCE: © 1999 Barbara L. McCombs, PhD. Not to be used without prior written permission from Dr. Barbara McCombs, Senior Research Scientist, Human Motivation, Learning, and Development, University of Denver's Research Institute, 2050 E. Iliff Avenue, Room 224, Denver, Colorado 80208-2616.

Seven Dimensions of Learning Power (Crick, 2006)

- changing and learning vs. being static or stuck
- critical curiosity vs. passivity
- meaning making vs. fragmentation
- creativity vs. rule-boundedness
- learning relationships/interdependence vs. isolation/dependence
- strategic awareness vs. behaving like a robot
- resilience vs. fragility

---

lifelong learner, do you think these dimensions might also apply to teachers? In our work, we believe they do. These dimensions may look different for teachers—they may show up in a variety of ways, just as they do for all of us as lifelong learners. One of the biggest factors that can influence where any of us may fall on the seven dimensions is how supportive our school context is in facilitating the lifelong learning of all people in the system. With this in mind, we invite you to look at yourself through the lens of the seven dimensions of lifelong learning in Activity 7.2.

A fundamental issue facing our nation's schools is that as many as 33% of new teachers leave within three years of entering the profession, and another 46% leave in the first five years (Rubalcava, 2005). The primary reason they leave is that the realities of everyday life in the classroom do not correspond with their visions of school. The teachers say there is a profound mismatch between their goals and the realities of everyday life in the classroom.

Many teachers enter the teaching profession because they want to connect with students as individuals, create a sense of community, and help students develop their personal creativity and talents. When Rubalcava (2005) asked teachers about their vision and what they actually encounter in schools, she found that their visions were very different from their actual experiences in schools. Specifically, Rubalcava asked new teachers to indicate how important these four goals of education are to them:

1. citizenship,
2. socialization,
3. economic efficiency, and
4. self-actualization.

New teachers picked self-actualization and socialization as carrying the greatest importance to them, but the current school agenda focuses almost exclusively on economic efficiency through an emphasis on testing, accountability, and predetermined content objectives. However, when schools emphasize learner-centered environments, Rubalcava found, teachers are able to balance current policies with a focus on nurturing their students' emotional health and creativity. In these learner-centered schools, the teachers engage students in critical thinking and creative expression, using strategies such as cultural exchanges, role playing, environmental projects, story writing, literature-based

ACTIVITY 7.2

Your Learning Power as an Educational Professional

Consider these seven dimensions of learning power as you think about yourself as a learner in your current job. Use the rating scale to rate yourself.

5 Powerful	3 In Between	1 Powerless
_____ changing and learning	_____	_____ being static or stuck
_____ critical curiosity	_____	_____ passivity
_____ meaning making	_____	_____ fragmentation
_____ creativity	_____	_____ rule-boundedness
_____ learning relationships/ interdependence	_____	_____ isolation/dependence
_____ strategic awareness	_____	_____ behaving like a robot
_____ resilience	_____	_____ fragility
_____ **Total 5s**	_____ **Total 3s**	_____ **Total 1s**

Where do most of your scores fall? Are they mostly 5s? 3s? 1s? Are there areas you could not easily rate? If so, why do you think that is true?

In the areas where you scored 5s, describe in your journal how you might collaborate with colleagues to spread the learning power you feel in those areas. In the areas where you scored 1s, describe in your journal at least one step for each area that you can take to move toward a score of 3, or even 5.

Now take a moment to consider this question: do your descriptions of how to share your learning power with colleagues and the steps you can take to improve your own learning power play a role in your vision for schools? Think carefully about your response and then record it in your journal.

SOURCE: © 1999 Barbara L. McCombs, PhD. Not to be used without prior written permission from Dr. Barbara McCombs, Senior Research Scientist, Human Motivation, Learning, and Development, University of Denver's Research Institute, 2050 E. Iliff Avenue, Room 224, Denver, Colorado 80208-2616.

learning, integrated physical education, and inquiry-based collaborative learning. For new teachers, connecting with each other and their students in a meaningful way means they are more likely to succeed with any of these strategies (Rubalcava, 2005).

On another note, because of the imbalance in the current focus of schools, many parents are deciding to homeschool their children to have better control over what their children are learning and to increase the relevance of what they are learning to their personal and social development (Coalition of Self-Learning, 2003). The number of students being homeschooled has grown from about 20,000 in 1980 to over 2 million in 2003. Their average test results are currently higher than those of their public school peers. Homeschooled students are also reported to have more self-confidence, creativity, optimism, and courage to explore, according to studies reported by the Coalition of Self-Learning (2003). These are the primary qualities of lifelong learners identified in studies done in the United Kingdom reported by Deakin Crick and McCombs (in press).

My Plan for a Learner-Centered Classroom

As you have reflected on your vision for schools, what are some of the things you can do to create a more learner-centered classroom? This is a good time to pause for a moment to reflect on what you have been thinking as you've read thus far and to connect what you have been reading to your own beliefs and practices. Using the questions the box below as a guide, write in your journal your thoughts about how you can proceed in making your classroom more learner centered.

After you have responded to the questions in the box below, we recommend as a next step devising ways to meet with some of your colleagues who are also interested in making their classrooms more learner centered. If your school is using the Assessment of Learner-Centered Practices Surveys,

---

Steps Toward a More Learner-Centered Classroom

1. What are your primary goals for making your classroom more learner centered? List some for your students and some for yourself.
2. What are the major steps you will need to take? List them in the order you think you will need to proceed—you can always modify as you go.
3. What specific activities and materials will you need to include in order to implement your plan?
4. List the resources (including time, money, materials) available to you now.
5. List any additional resources you will need in order to implement your plan.

---

you may already have had opportunities to meet to discuss how to use the ALCP surveys on your journey to becoming learner centered. Or, if several of you are reading this book and have completed the mini-surveys in Activity 2.1 and Activity 7.2, you may want to arrange to meet to discuss your experiences and the reflections you have recorded in your journaling. Through joining and collaborating with like-minded colleagues, you can increase the likelihood of effecting change, not only in your own classroom, but throughout your school.

How Can I Manage Resistance to Change?

One of the most important lessons we learned in implementing the LCM in dozens of schools and districts is that people will change when they are ready. Just as with learning, you can't mandate change. However, you can make it invitational, intriguing, and meaningful from the individual's perspective. In fact, what we learned from our review of the literature on change is that there are fundamental principles of change (McCombs & Whisler, 1997), shown in Figure 7.8.

Try this mind experiment: Replace the word "change" with "learning" for each of these principles. You will discover that the principles apply either to "learning" or to "change," in spite of the sometimes awkward wording. Learning and change are, in fact, flip sides of the same psychological process—each is about "changing your mind," quite literally!

Resistance to change is what people do naturally when they are fearful or feel insecure. When we feel these emotions, keeping things the same acts as a security blanket to keep us safe and on familiar ground. When we feel afraid or insecure, resisting change is a valid choice. Sometimes we believe that change is simply unnecessary, but, at a deeper level, we may unconsciously not want to disrupt our comfort zone. When we are acting as change agents and facilitators of learning, we have to trust that people will come along when they are ready, just as you know that your students will change—that is, learn—when they are ready.

Another helpful thing we have learned is that in any area of personal change, for the change process to be successful, there are some clear stages that individuals go through, as shown in Figure 7.9.

First, all change begins with a perceived crisis that instills a sense of the need to change. At this initial stage, people need the crisis because it helps develop an awareness that a change is needed. The crisis helps us generate a will to change and to take ownership of the need to change. To be supported at this stage, we need a sense of hope that it is possible for us to make the change that is needed.

At the second stage, even though the will and need to change have been acknowledged, most of us find it difficult to move forward until we can observe others—like ourselves—who have been able to make the change that is needed. At this stage, we need the support of seeing different models we can identify with, and we need to talk with others about the specifics—the what and the how—of the change process.

At the third stage, even though we understand what is needed and have seen the change modeled and explained, we still need to make it our own. We need coaching and mentoring support

Figure 7.8   Principles of Learning and Change

Principles of Learning and Change

In living systems, change and learning are flip sides of the same psychological processes. Each is characterized by a transformation in thinking, each is engaged in at a personal level, and each is based on research-validated principles of human learning, motivation, and development. The following principles represent what we know about personal and organizational change. They are grouped into the three domains present in all living systems: personal, technical, and organizational.

Personal Domain

- Change is a new way of thinking—it starts in the hearts and minds of individuals and results in seeing learning and learners differently.
- Change is seen differently by different people—to be successful, it must be built on areas of agreement.
- Focusing on learners and learning creates a common vision and direction for change.
- Change begins with hope—believing it is possible.
- Change requires permission to make mistakes and engage in conflict resolution and negotiation skills.

Technical Domain

- Substantive change seeks answers to perplexing issues and must be supported by opportunities for inquiry, dialogue, learning, reflection, and practice.
- Honoring the learner's ability to make choices about and control his or her own learning facilitates change.
- Change occurs when each person sees himself or herself as a learner and sees change as basically a learning process.
- Like learning, change is a lifelong and continuous process.
- A critical outcome of the change process is the creation of learning communities that enhance, support, and sustain the motivation for ongoing learning and change.

Organizational Domain

- Change is facilitated when individuals feel personally empowered by feelings of ownership, respect, personal support and trust.
- Key stakeholders must be involved in the change and know precisely what is to be changed.
- Like learning, change occurs best when it is invitational and not mandated.
- Change requires commitment of resources, including time, knowledge, and leadership skills.
- Change is facilitated by leaders who share power, facilitate communication, and are inclusive of all learners.

SOURCE: Copyright © 1999 Barbara L. McCombs, PhD, Senior Research Scientist, University of Denver Research Institute, 2050 E. Iliff Avenue, Boettcher East – Room 224, Denver, CO 80208.

---

strategies to tailor the classroom practice strategies we have seen, try them out, and revise them as needed. It is at this point that real ownership occurs, and we can begin to develop personal responsibility for an ongoing process of continuous learning and change.

Finally, the fourth stage ensures successful change when we engage in ongoing self-assessment, networking with others who are implementing learner-centered strategies, and building learner-centered support groups and learning communities that can help us adopt and sustain the attitudes of continuous learning and change. We need ongoing and personalized professional development that supports us as individuals and supports the community as a whole.

Figure 7.9   Stages of Personal Change

Stage 1: Developing Awareness, Will to Change, and Ownership of Need to Change—Showing change is possible, inspiring hope.

Stage 2: Observing Models and Building Understanding of Personal Domain Practices—Seeing different models, discussing "what and how."

Stage 3: Adapting Strategies, Building Skills, and Developing Personal Responsibility for Continuous Learning and Change—Tailoring strategies, coaching, trying out, revising.

Stage 4: Adopting and Sustaining Attitudes and Practices That Contribute to Continuous Learning—Ongoing self-assessment, networking, support.

The box below summarizes what we know about helping people change. As you continue your journey through your own changes toward learner-centered practices, and as you help others begin or renew their own learner-centered journey, you can refer to this summary as a shorthand way to refresh your memory and support your own process.

Obtaining the Necessary Support for Learner-Centered Schools

As you discovered when you engaged in the exercise in the box below regarding your goals and vision for schools and the resources necessary for you to realize those goals, you began identifying

---

Learner-Centered Processes That Best Facilitate Change

- Invite people into the change process. Remember, change can't be mandated!
- Begin with the people who are the most interested. Build numbers from that core group. Remember that change in living systems occurs because of critical relationships—not critical mass!
- Include people with divergent and diverse viewpoints to enliven the discussions and build authentic consensus. Remember that we learn the most from people whose views differ the most from our own. Engaging in respectful dialogue is the most likely way to build consensus.
- Trust that people will come to the change process when they are ready. Trying to hurry their process will likely produce more resistance, not less. Address resistance openly as a natural human process. Examine what is producing the resistance. Remember that learning and change are flip sides of the same psychological process; sometimes people just have to feel free of fear before they can take that first step.
- Build opportunities for people to make connections and to provide support for each other. Remember that both learning and change are supported by positive relationships and support systems.
- Use the LCPs to align instructional practices across the domains of learning. Remember that the LCPs are the foundation for holistic and systemic change across domains of human learning and across domains of living systems function.

specific processes, materials, people, practices, and policies that are necessary for developing a learner-centered school. As we pointed out then, as an individual teacher, you can certainly make a difference, but your impact can be so much greater when you can be joined by other teachers in your building.

The ideal solution is to involve administrators and parents by showing them that they are primary stakeholders. In our work with the ALCP Surveys in schools and districts, we have learned that building communities of learners is at the heart of helping schools become learner centered. Although the change may start with individual teachers, spreading the word and learning together with colleagues at the building level provides the critical mass necessary to begin the change process.

Becoming learner centered requires various types of support. One of the most important is for the school and/ or district to recognize and attend to the needs of teachers as learners. Specifically, the school and/or district must design processes and structures that provide the following:

- Teacher mentoring and peer assistance. To grow and change, teachers need to know they will get mentoring and assistance from their colleagues and peers.
- Collaboration and peer review. To be able to continually evaluate and improve their practices, teachers need to be able to collaborate with colleagues, participate in reviewing them, and feel comfortable having their peers review their instructional practices. The goal is to set up a system that is positive and constructive, allows for diverse and multiple perspectives, and promotes professional learning communities.

- Voice and responsibility in their own learning and accountability processes. Just as students profit from owning their own learning and improvement processes, teachers also need to have voice in how and what they are learning and how their learning and performance should be assessed. While voice and responsibility confer ownership, they also offer the opportunity to set up accountability practices that are empowering and positive rather than mandated and fear-based.

- Professional learning communities. When teachers feel they are part of a professional learning community that is vital, positive, caring, and based on learner-centered principles, the joy of learning and change returns. Participating in learning communities provides the vital personal connections and relationships that are at the heart of learning and change.

- Real-world, inquiry-based training and contexts for bringing new teachers into the process. The most powerful teacher learning and development models are those that allow teachers to follow their own inquiry into the questions they most want to answer to improve their practices and reach more students. This means that teachers need learning experiences that are meaningful and relevant from their perspective. It also means that these learning experiences must provide opportunities for experienced and new teachers to work together and be connected to opportunities to also work with students in nearby teacher education programs.

How best to meet these needs of teachers as learners? Of prime importance is for the school and/or district to design structures and processes that support personal changes, including the following:

- Establishing department- or grade-level support groups. One of the first steps for teachers to feel comfortable as learners is for them to develop trust and feelings of safety in sharing their areas of strength as well as areas in which they wish to improve. We have learned that one of the most effective ways to promote this trust and safety is to establish support groups at the department, team, or grade level. Within the structure of the support group, ALCP feedback can be used as a way to focus on the most effective strategies for changing particular areas of practice or particular teacher beliefs and characteristics.
- Changing time structures to allow for interdisciplinary or cross-department meetings. Once the comfort level of teachers has been ensured, we have learned, they are empowered to work on ways to change the time structures within the school calendar to allow for meeting with colleagues in other departments or disciplines. This allows them to expand their repertoire of effective

practices across content areas and with diverse students.
- Implementing coaching and mentoring strategies for pairing faculty members. Our work with teachers has shown that as teachers in support groups identify those teachers who are most effectively reaching students in all the areas of learner-centered practice, the group begins to identify those who can become coaches and mentors for others wishing to improve in these areas. This process is a fundamental example of what Fullan (2002) has called "building capacity from within." What it shows is that the best experts are those teachers who are most effective with particular students, particular areas of practice, or particular content areas. In our work we have learned that we, as outside experts, are helpful in providing the latest evidence-based practices and explaining the LCM and its assessment tools, ALCP Surveys. We become the facilitators who empower teachers (and others) to begin the learner-centered journey and to identify the expertise that resides in their school buildings. We help everyone in the building recognize that the best experts are already in their building. The goal for coaches and mentors is to find ways to bring the existing expertise to the surface and help teachers share effective practice in ways that create critical relationships and caring, learner-centered learning communities. Another of our goals is to help teachers (and administrators) see that all

teachers in a system are experts in at least one area of practice. What we want to help them do is to create a total learning system that includes all teachers (and, of course, their students!).

- Rewarding those who produce desired student outcomes. Although researchers have mixed views on the value of external rewards (e.g., Kohn, 2005), most agree that if rewards are tied to the values and goals defined by the vision of the kind of student outcomes teachers (and the whole school community) want to produce, well-designed reward strategies can propel people to even higher levels of excellence. Some successful systems we have seen include special celebrations, social events, honors, or opportunities for pursuing advanced degrees. The successful systems tie the rewards to student outcomes and get students involved in the celebration process. Well-designed reward systems address the central goal in the learner-centered journey: helping teachers know they are making a difference in the lives and learning of their students.

We have seen that once supports are in place for personal change, teachers are empowered to take on leadership roles that move these changes toward more learner-centered practices to the department, school, or even district levels. These leadership roles include the following:

1. Providing intensive training in learner-centered theory and practices in department or grade-level groups. As with personal change, people first need to understand the LCPs and LCM, its ALCP survey tools, and other supportive processes. To be most effective, this needs to be done in a motivational and invitational way.

2. Empowering departments or grade-level groups to access resources across the school or district. As faculty meet within and across departments, they have the opportunity to identify the resources they need to become more learner centered. Leadership teams can be established, and all involved can be encouraged to "think outside the box" to define the professional development, materials, and other resources they need to ensure the success of their journey.

3. Providing opportunities for cross-department or cross-grade-level support groups for sharing successful change strategies. Just as the within-department or grade-level sharing supports personal as well as systemic change, taking these strategies to the next level promotes learning and change across the entire system. Our observation of these cross-department and cross-grade-level support groups is that when the process is inclusive and invitational, the participants learn the most from those whose opinions differ the most from their own.

4. Providing for dialogue and connections with model programs. Providing a forum for respectful dialogue is essential. All facultyru: need to feel safe to share their views, know they will be listened to, and to know that all views will be respected.

Once this culture of learning and caring is established, what emerges is an opportunity to use the combined creativity of the entire faculty, staff, and students to define learning opportunities that move beyond school walls. This may take the form of field trips to see new models of learner-centered practice that are particularly effective, visiting institutions of higher education to learn the latest evidence-based practices, or talking with a variety of experts who can infuse new ideas and thinking into school and classroom practices. Using the foundation of the LCPs and evidence-based practices we have set out in this book provides a framework for thinking about and evaluating those programs, practices, and policies most likely to produce the changes we most want: students and faculty who are mutually engaged in continuous, lifelong learning and growth.

Where Do I Go From Here?

Time now for a final set of reflections. Gather the journal entries you have made as you've made your way through this book. The box on page 144 lists the various reflections and activities from all the chapters.

Using your journal entries as a guide, construct a summary of what you have learned by responding to the following questions:

1. What does it mean to be learner centered?

2. What are two (or more) effects learner-centered practices have on students?

3. How do learner-centered practices affect the achievement gap?

4. How have my beliefs about learners, learning, and/or teaching changed as I have read this book and reflected on my beliefs and practices?

5. What are my primary goals for students as I move toward being more learner centered?

6. What are my primary goals for myself as I move toward being more learner centered?

7. What are my primary goals for my school as I move toward being more learner centered?

8. What are the first three things I need to do to continue becoming more learner centered?

9. Who are the colleagues most likely to collaborate with me in becoming more learner centered?

10. Who are the administrators most likely to provide support and resources for becoming more learner centered?

Our hope is that your responding to these questions validates your personal goals and values and forms the beginning (or the continuing) of a learning process for you that leads you toward more learner-centered beliefs and practices. We know that your journey will be unique (everyone's is!) and rewarding. Enjoy the process, and please invite others to join you on the journey.

Best wishes, Barbara and Lynda.

P.S. Here's another puzzle for you to ponder as you continue your journey. As you consider how you might solve this puzzle, reflect on whether your approach has changed since you began reading this book. You'll see that we've given you a few more hints in this puzzle. If your approach has changed, how would you describe what you are doing now in comparison with what you did to solve the puzzles in Chapter 1? And, now that you've read the book, how would you try to teach someone to solve puzzles like these?

Summary of Reflections, Exercises, and Activities

Chapter 1

- Your reflections about how you went about figuring out the puzzle picture on page 2.

- Your answers to the questions on pages 3–4 about how you typically

  – reduce stress,
  – play,
  – think about and plan events and activities in your life,
  – approach problems, and
  – approach learning something new.

- Your answers to these questions regarding teaching your students how to solve the puzzle picture on page 2.

  – How would you construct a lesson (or lessons) that incorporates what you've learned so far about Learner-Centered Practices?
  – How would your lesson (or lessons) reflect your own learning strategies that you used to figure out the picture?

Chapter 2

- Your scores on the Mini-Assessment on page 26 and how they compare with the Learner-Centered Rubric on page 28.

Chapter 3

- Your answers to these questions on page 42 regarding your beliefs about learners, learning, and teaching:

  – Do I know how my students perceive my teaching practices?
  – Do I really believe that all students are capable learners?
  – What do I want to do to reach those students who seem "difficult" to me?
  – What are my fears about developing learning partnerships with my students?

- Your observations of the "Getting to Know You" activity on page 43.

Chapter 4

- The activities you generated for each of the 14 Learner-Centered Principles.

- Your reflections during Exercise 4.1 (page 68) regarding what the Learner-Centered Principles mean to you.

- Your reflections during Exercise 4.2 (page 69) about what is and is not "learner centered."

Chapter 5

- Your thoughts and reflections about Ferrero's questions on page 71:

  - What motivated me to go into teaching?
  - What do I think students should know and be able to do?
  - Who are the influences on my education philosophy?
  - Which colleagues share my vision?
  - What do parents, students, and local citizens want, need, and believe?

- Your responses to the exercise about addressing the achievement gap on page 85:

  - Have you or anyone in your school asked the students what they think are the reasons for low achievement? If so, how well do their responses match those we described in the previous section? If not, what do you think they would say?
  - You may wish to design an interview format to use in collecting their views regarding the factors underlying low achievement. You may also wish to include questions designed to learn what the students believe are the factors contributing to high achievement.

Chapter 6

- Your self-rating of how often you think you implement the practices shown in Figure 6.3 on page 99 used by learner-centered teachers.

- Changes you would be comfortable making to begin implementing some (or all) of these practices.

- The insights you recorded after reading the chapter.

Chapter 7

- Your reflections about how you approached solving the puzzle picture on page 2 in Chapter 1:

  - Did you feel a sense of closure?
  - Were you interested in the details of why the puzzle is difficult for most people?
  - Did you share the puzzle with anyone else? If so, did you teach them how to solve it? Did you enjoy that teaching?
  - Would you like to see how you'd do with another, similar puzzle now that you have learned how to solve the first one? If so, what would you do differently this time?

- Activity 7.1 on page 130 in which you took another version of the Teacher Mini-Survey and compared your score against the Learner-Centered Rubric.

- Your thoughts on what you believe would be the characteristics of the best schools (page 130).

- Your thoughts on re-assessing your vision for schools (see the box on page 135).

Resource A

Teacher Strategy Ideas

Elementary and Middle School Ideas

Creative Name Tag

Draw what you do well. | Draw what you like to do.

Draw a value. | List 4 words that are you.

SOURCE: Dr. H. Jerome Freiberg, University of Houston, Consistency Management and Cooperative Discipline Department (1995). Used with permission.

Hearing Student Voices

1. About Me	• My nickname is • I am in the ____ grade. • I have ____ brothers and sisters.
2. My Favorites	• My favorite school subject is • My favorite thing to do at school is
3. How I Feel About School	• I would like school to help me • If I could learn anything at school, I would like to learn
4. How I Feel About Teachers	• A good teacher is one who • My teacher thinks it is important to
5. About My Neighborhood	• Good things that happen in my neighborhood are • People I like best in my neighborhood are
6. About My Family	• What I like best about my family is
7. How I Learn Best	• I learn best when I • Activities in class that do not help me learn are

SOURCE: Dr. H. Jerome Freiberg, University of Houston, Consistency Management and Cooperative Discipline Department (1995). Used with permission.

High School Ideas

Freshman English: Mr. Hirsch

Small Group Attitude Survey

Name: _____   Period: _____

Please select the THREE (3) statements that best characterize your feelings about working in small groups. Although you may agree with many of the statements, only check off the **three** that are most representative of your feelings about small group work.

When I am in a small group, I

_____ like to be the leader.

_____ feel like I do all the work.

_____ wish I could work alone instead.

_____ feel guilty because I do not want to work as hard as others.

_____ would rather socialize in my group than work.

_____ can't get a word in because everyone else is talking.

_____ am worried that people will not like my ideas.

_____ think others are uncooperative and hard to get along with.

_____ prefer to let others take the lead.

_____ am the cheerleader helping keep everyone motivated and interested.

_____ say to myself that I hate small groups.

_____ say to myself that I like small groups.

Johnson's Awareness Quotient

Name _____   Year in school _____

Siblings
  Names and ages _____

_____

_____

Who I live with _____

Pets _____

Favorites _____

  food _____

  movie _____

  music _____

  restaurant _____

  snack _____

  TV show _____

Average hours per week I spend on academics/homework _____

Is there one night that seems more overloaded than others?_____

Favorite subjects and why

  1. _____

  2. _____

  3. _____

Rank your skills from 1 to 10 (10 = highest) in the following areas

reading _____   athletics _____   creativity _____

writing _____   drama _____   visual arts _____

speaking _____   time mgmt _____   note taking _____

listening _____   friendship _____   musical arts _____

science _____   leadership_____   independence _____

math _____   interdependence _____

Extracurriculars I am currently involved in _____

_____

Average time I spend per week _____

_____

_____

Extracurriculars I hope to be involved in this year _____

_____

_____

Average time I will spend per week_____

_____

_____

Work

    where _____

    average hours per week _____

    responsibilities include _____

    When I have free time, I like to spend it with _____

    and/or by doing _____

I'd rather spend free time with my friends ___ or alone ___ Why? _____

_____

_____

Community services I'm involved with_____

_____

_____

Volunteering I do _____

Family obligations_____

_____

_____

Anything else that occupies your time? Share_____

_____

_____

Any post–high school plans_____

if college, ideas for major _____

if work, what field _____

if other, explain _____

Current course schedule _____

EB	_____	Teacher	_____
1st	_____	Teacher	_____
2nd	_____	Teacher	_____
3rd	_____	Teacher	_____
4th	_____	Teacher	_____
5th	_____	Teacher	_____
6th	_____	Teacher	_____
7th	_____	Teacher	_____
8th	_____	Teacher	_____
9th	_____	Teacher	_____

NOTE: The Small Group Attitude Survey and Johnson's Awareness Quotient were supplied by teachers at the Illinois High School District #113. In the Small Group Attitude Survey, the teacher uses student responses to organize students into diverse learning groups that can then be switched based on student input. Johnson's Awareness Quotient helps teachers get to know their students personally and academically.

Resource B

Contacts: Learner-Centered Projects and Schools

Dr. Ruth Deakin Crick, University of Bristol, England: Ruth.Deakin-Crick@bristol.ac.uk

Developed the Effective Lifelong Learning Inventory (ELLI) for Grades 4–12 in the United States and comparable grades in the United Kingdom Can be contacted for additional materials and information about ELLI and the seven dimensions of Learning Power.

Dr. Marcia Mentkowski, Director of Research and Evaluation, Alverno College, Milwaukee, Wisconsin: marcia.mentkowski@alverno.edu

A contact for learning about Alverno's Ability-Based Learning Program. This program is aligned with the APA Learner-Centered Psychological Principles and provides K–20 teachers with guidelines for developing and assessing meaningful, multidisciplinary student learning outcomes.

Dr. Janell Cleland, Director of Learning, Illinois Township District #113, Deerfield, Illinois: JCleland@dist113.org

The district has been aligning its practices to the APA Learner-Centered Psychological Principles for over seven years. They are working with Dr. Barbara McCombs to deepen their journey to learner-centered practices. Teachers at the two high schools in this district are exceptional in learner-centered classroom practices across discipline areas.

Susan Espinoza, Development Director, San Antonio State College, Texas: sespinoz@accd.edu

This community college system is a prime example of learner-centered practices for students leaving traditional school systems and needing developmentally appropriate curricula. Faculty are using the Assessment of Learner-Centered Practices (ALCP) college-level instructor and student surveys to deepen their journey to learner-centered classroom practices.

Dr. Dennis Harper, Founder and CEO, Generation YES, Olympia, Washington: dennis@genyes.org

Developed this award-winning program for students in upper elementary through college. The Gen YES program pairs students with teachers in the implementation of technology in the teaching and learning process. This program is aligned with the APA Learner-Centered Psychological Principles and is highly cost-effective as well as related to increased student social and learning outcomes.

Resource C

Books and Journals Worth a Read

Books

Arnold, W. (2005). *No child undiscovered.* Coral Springs, FL: Llumina Press.

Blankstein, A. (2005). *Failure is not an option: Six principles that guide student achievement in high-performing schools.* Thousand Oaks, CA: Corwin Press.

Boynton, M., & Boynton, C. (2005). *The educator's guide to preventing and solving discipline problems.* Alexandria, VA: SCD [ASCD].

Deakin Crick, R. (2006). *Learning power in practice: A guide for teachers.* Thousand Oaks, CA: Corwin Press.

Goldman, G., & Newman, J. B. (1998). *Empowering students to transform schools.* Thousand Oaks, CA: Corwin Press.

Mills, R., & Spittle, E. (2001). *The wisdom within.* Auburn, WA: Lone Pine.

Mills-Naim, A. C. (2005). *The spark within: A special book for youth.* Auburn, WA: Lone Pine.

Riordan, T., & Roth, J. (Eds.). (2005). *Disciplines as frameworks for student learning: Teaching the practice of the disciplines.* Sterling, VA: Stylus.

Vryhof, S. C. (2004). *Between memory and vision.* Cambridge, UK: William B. Eerdmans.

Journals and Periodic Publications

Educational Leadership. Published for educators by Association for Supervision and Curriculum Development: www.ascd.org

Edutopia. Publication of the George Lucas Educational Foundation: www.glef.org

Phi Delta Kappan. Published for educators by Phi Delta Kappa International, Inc.: www.pdkintl.org/kappan

NOTE: All of these recommendations are consistent with the Learner-Centered Model, Principles, and Practices. They extend our thinking about what is possible.

Resource D

Learner-Centered Glossary: Some Definitions

Culture: The dynamic, deeply learned confluence of language, values, beliefs, and behaviors that pervade every aspect of a person's (and/or organization's) life (Wlodkowski & Ginsberg, 1995). Also refers to the operating norms of any group or organization that reflect different values, beliefs, and so on, of that group.

Domains of Change: Aspects of living systems that occur simultaneously at various levels of system functioning. In educational systems, the levels of functioning are classroom, school, district, community, and society. The domains of change operating throughout all these levels are

- *personal,* which supports the personal, motivational/learning, and interpersonal needs of those who serve and/or are served by the system (e.g., students, teachers, administrators, parents);
- *organizational,* which provides the organizational and management structures and policies that support the personal and technical domains and, ultimately, learning and achievement for all learners; and
- *technical,* which specifies the content and performance standards, curriculum structures and processes, instructional approaches, and assessment strategies that best promote learning and achievement of all students and learners in the system.

Honoring the Person as an Individual: The belief that individual learners are unique and learn best when this uniqueness is honored and accommodated. Individual differences include

- cultural heritage,
- gender,
- profiles of intelligences,
- socioeconomic status,
- educational background,
- family structure and dynamics,
- life experiences and their interactions for each person.

Intrinsic Motivation: Motivation inherent in human beings. It naturally emerges and flourishes in learner-centered contexts.

Learner-Centered(ness): Respecting the person as a learner and honoring the person as an individual. Holding beliefs, attitudes, practices, principles, and so on that reflect the assumptions and principles of the *Learner-Centered Psychological Principles:*

- learners are unique, and this uniqueness must be respected and attended to;
- learning is holistic and constructive in nature;
- a positive social context and relationships enhance learning; and
- learning and motivation are natural processes for all learners.

Learner-Centered Practices: Teaching and learning approaches, processes, communication styles, and school and classroom management strategies that are consistent with the Learner-Centered Principles and definition of "learner-centeredness."

Learner-Centered Psychological Principles: Fourteen principles that summarize findings from a century of research on learning and learners. The Principles were produced by the American Psychological Association's (APA) Presidential Task Force on Psychology in Education and the Mid-continent Regional Educational Laboratory, and published in January 1993 and revised and published by the APA in 1997. The principles are categorized into four domains of factors impacting learning for each individual:

- Metacognitive and Cognitive,
- Motivational and Affective,
- Developmental and Social, and
- Individual Differences.

Lifelong Learners: People who value and are committed to ongoing learning and growth throughout the lifespan, understanding that learning is change and change is learning.

Living Systems: A description of systems whose fundamental goal is to serve humans and their unique needs and capacities (e.g., educational, family, and social systems); those systems whose operation is best understood by principles describing the particular processes relevant to the functions and purposes of the system. For educational systems, processes are related to learning and the individual learner across personal, technical, and organizational domains.

Personal Change Process: A transformation process in which there is a substantial and sustainable change in beliefs, attitudes, knowledge, emotions, and behaviors, resulting in a "shift" in practice. Begins with the individual and progresses to the group or cultural level. Stages in the personal change process include four phases:

1. developing awareness, will to change, and ownership of need to change;

2. observing models and building understanding of personal domain practices;

3. adapting strategies, building skills, and developing personal responsibility for continuous learning and change; and

4. adopting and maintaining attitudes and practices that contribute to continuous learning and professional development.

Psychology of Learning and Psychology of Change: Understanding that change and learning are synonymous and occur within the "heads and hearts" of individuals as a result of transformations in thinking, feeling, and behaving.

Respecting the Person as a Learner: The belief that *all individuals learn and are motivated to learn* when their basic capacities, talents, abilities, and needs are known, respected, and accommodated in supportive teaching and learning practices. The most important accommodations include providing opportunities for

- personal choice,
- control,
- connections,
- responsibility
- cooperation,
- competence,
- voice,
- respect,
- trust,
- relevance, and
- challenge.

Systemic Change: Shifts in society, organizations, and individual behavior that occur as a result of the dynamic patterns of thinking and relationships between people and their environment. Change in one domain of a system automatically and always results in changes in other domains of that system. A holistic and comprehensive way of thinking about and bringing about change through the simultaneous consideration of the personal, technical, and organizational domains of living systems.

Transformation: A process in which a fundamental shift in understanding emerges that results in a new way of thinking, feeling, and behaving; occurs in response to significant experiences that alter existing perceptions and understandings.

Voice: Each individual's expression of thoughts, feelings, and interpretations or perceptions of reality at any point in time; an expression of uniqueness that must be honored and respected in learning.

Whole Person: A term that acknowledges all aspects of a person: physical, social, emotional, intellectual, and spiritual.

References

Alexander, P. A., & Murphy, P. K. (1998). The research base for APA's learner-centered psychological principles. In N. Lambert & B. L. McCombs (Eds.), *How students learn: Reforming schools through learner-centered education.* Washington, DC: American Psychological Association.

Alvarez, H. K., & Ollendick, T. H. (2004/2005). Addressing aggressive behavior in schools: Arming the educator. *On the Move with School-Based Mental Health, 9*(2), 1–2, 4–6.

American Educational Research Association. (2004). Closing the gap: High achievement for students of color. *Research Points, 2*(3), 1–4.

Amrein, A. L., & Berliner, D. C. (2003). The effects of high-stakes testing on student motivation and learning. *Educational Leadership, 60*(5), 32–38.

APA Task Force on Psychology in Education. (1993, January). *Learner-centered psychological principles: Guidelines for school redesign and reform.* Washington, DC: American Psychological Association and Mid-Continent Regional Educational Laboratory.

APA Work Group of the Board of Educational Affairs. (1997, November). *Learner-centered psychological principles: A framework for school reform and redesign.* Washington, DC: American Psychological Association.

Battistich, V., Soloman, D., Watson, M., & Schaps, E. (1997). Caring school communities. *Educational Psychologist, 32*(3), 137–151.

Berliner, D. (2005, April). *Ignoring the forest, blaming the trees: Our impoverished view of educational reform.* AERA distinguished lecture at the annual meeting of the American Educational Research Association, Montreal.

Biglan, A., Mrazek, P. J., Carnine, D., & Flay, B. R. (2003). The integration of research and practice in the prevention of youth problem behaviors. *American Psychologist, 58*(6/7), 433–440.

Blum, R. W. (2005). A case for school connectedness. *Educational Leadership, 62*(7), 16–20.

Borko, H. (2004). Professional development and teacher learning: Mapping the terrain. *Educational Researcher, 33*(8), 13–15.

Borko, H., Peressini, D., Romagnano, L., Knuth, E., Willis-Yorker, C., Wooley, C., et al. (2000). Teacher education does matter: A situative view of learning to teach secondary mathematics. *Educational Psychologist, 35*(3), 193–206.

Borman, G. D., & Overman, L. T. (2004). Academic resilience in mathematics among poor and minority students. *Elementary School Journal, 104*, 177–195.

Bracey, G. W. (2002). International comparisons: An excuse to avoid meaningful educational reform. *Education Week, 21*(19), 30–32.

Bransford, J. D., Brown, A. L., & Cocking, R. R. (1999). *How people learn: Brain, mind, experience, and school.* Washington, DC: National Research Council.

Brendtro, L. K. (1999, June). *Tools for reclaiming at-risk youth.* Keynote presentation at the 8th Annual Rocky Mountain Regional Conference in Violence Prevention in Schools and Communities, Denver.

Bryk, A. S., & Schneider, B. (2003). Trust in schools: A core resource for school reform. *Educational Leadership, 60*(6), 40–44.

Cacioppo, J. T., Hawkley, L. C., Rickett, E. M., & Masi, C. M. (2005). Sociality, spirituality, and meaning making: Chicago health, aging, and social relations study. *Review of General Psychology, 9*(2), 143–155.

Caine, R. N., & Caine, G. (1997). *Education on the edge of possibility.* Alexandria, VA: Association for Supervision and Curriculum Development.

Calvert, M. (2002, April). *Raising voices in school: The impact of young decision makers on schools and youth organizations.* Paper presented at the annual meeting of the American Educational Research Association, New Orleans.

Carey, K. (2003, October). *Teacher effectiveness presentation.* Planning meeting at the Joyce Foundation.

Carter, G. R. (2004). *The high stakes of school safety. Is it good for the kids?* Retrieved September 22, 2004, from http://www.ascd.org/portal/site/ascd/index.jsp/

Chrisman, V. (2005). How schools sustain success. *Educational Leadership, 62*(5), 16–21.

Coalition of Self-Learning. (2003). Life-long learning. *Learning Cooperatives Quarterly, 2*(1), 1–2. Available at http://www.creatinglearningcommunities.org/resources/lifelonglearning.htm

Cochran-Smith, M., & Zeichner, K. M. (2005). *Studying teacher education: The report of the AERA Panel on Research and Teacher Education.* Mahweh, NJ: Erlbaum.

Collins, V. (2005, April). *Improving achievement for students in poverty: A forum.* Presentation at the annual meeting of the Association for Supervision and Curriculum Development, Orlando, FL.

Combs, A. W. (1986). What makes a good helper? A person-centered approach. *Person-Centered Review, 1*(1), 51–61.

Combs, A. W. (1991). *The schools we need: New assumptions for educational reform.* Lanham, MD: University Press of America.

Combs, A. W., Miser, A. B., & Whitaker, K. S. (1999). *On becoming a school leader: A person-centered challenge.* Alexandria, VA: ASCD.

Comer, J. P. (2005). Child and adolescent development: The critical missing focus in school reform. *Phi Delta Kappan, 86*(10), 757–763.

Cook-Sather, A. (2002). Authorizing students' perspectives: Toward trust, dialogue, and change in education. *Educational Researcher, 31*(4), 3–14.

Corbett, D., Wilson, B., & Williams, B. (2005). No choice but success. *Educational Leadership, 62*(6), 8–12.

Crabtree, S. (2004, June 4). Teachers who care get most from kids. *The Detroit News.* Retrieved June 4, 2004, from http://www.detnews.com/2004/schools/0406/04/a09-172712.htm

Daniels, D. H., Kalkman, D. L., & McCombs, B. L. (2001). Individual differences in young children's perspectives on learning and teacher practices: Effects of learner-centered contexts on motivation. *Early Education and Development, 12*(2), 253–273.

Daniels, E. (2005). On the minds of middle schoolers. *Educational Leadership, 62*(7), 52–54.

Darling-Hammond, L. (1996). The quiet revolution: Rethinking teacher development. *Educational Leadership, 53*(6), 4–10.

Darling-Hammond, L. (1997). *The right to learn: A blueprint for creating schools that work.* San Francisco: Jossey-Bass.

Davis, H. A. (2006). Exploring the contexts of relationship quality between middle school students and teachers. *Elementary School Journal, 106*(3), 193–224.

Day, C. (2002). The challenge to be the best: Reckless curiosity and mischievous motivation. *Teachers and teaching: Theory and Practice, 8*(3/4), 421–434.

Deakin Crick, R., & McCombs, B. L. (in press). The assessment of learner-centered practices surveys (ALCPs): An English case study. Submitted to the *Research and Evaluation Journal.*

Deci, E. L., & Ryan, R. M. (1991). A motivational approach to self: Integration in personality. In R. Dienstbier (Ed.), *Nebraska symposium on motivation. Vol. 38. Perspectives on motivation* (pp. 237–288). Lincoln: University of Nebraska Press.

Dewey, J. (1938). *Experience and education.* New York: Macmillan.

Diamond, L. (2005, July 28). Testing law baffles parents. *The Atlanta Journal Constitution,* p. C1.

Diamond, M., & Hopson, J. (1998). *Magic trees of the mind.* New York: Dutton.

Dillon, S. (2004, July 21). When students are in flux, schools are in crisis. *The New York Times,* p. B9.

Doll, B., Zucker, S., & Brehm, K. (2004). *Resilient classrooms: Creating healthy environments for learning.* New York: Guilford.

DuFour, R. (1999, Fall). Living with paradox. *Association for Supervision and Curriculum Development Professional Development Newsletter,* 1–2. Alexandria, VA: Association for Supervision and Curriculum Development.

DuFour, R. (2004). What is a "professional learning community?" *Educational Leadership, 61*(8), 6–11.

Eisner, E. (2005). Back to whole. *Educational Leadership, 63*(1), 14–18.

Emerick, S., Hirsch, E., & Berry, B. (2004). Does highly qualified mean high-quality? *ASCD Infobrief, 39,* 1–10.

Ericson, D. P., & Ellet, F. S., Jr. (2002, April). *The question of the student in educational reform.* Paper presented at the annual meeting of the American Educational Research Association, New Orleans.

Fabes, R., & Martin, C. L. (2003). *Exploring child development* (2nd ed.). Boston: Pearson International.

Feistritzer, C. E. (1999, November). *The making of a teacher: A report on teacher preparation in the U.S.* Available at http://www.ncei.com/MakingTeacher-blts.htm

Ferrero, D. J. (2005). Pathways to reform: Start with values. *Educational Leadership, 62*(5), 8–14.

Fielding, M. (2000). The person-centered school. *Forum, 42*(2), 51–54.

Fielding, M. (2001). Students as radical agents of change. *Journal of Educational Change, 2*(3), 123–141.

Fielding, M. (2002a). *Beyond the rhetoric of student voice: New departures or new constraints in the transformation of 21st century schooling?* Paper presented as part of the International Symposium on "Student Voices and Democracy in Schools" at the annual meeting of the American Educational Research Association, New Orleans.

Fielding, M. (2002b). *Transformative approaches to student voice: Theoretical underpinning, recalcitrant realities.* Paper submitted to the McGill Journal of Education.

Flock, L., Repetti, R., & Ullman, J. (2005). Classroom social experiences as predictors of academic performance. *Developmental Psychology, 41*(2), 319–327.

Forbes, S. (1999). *Holistic education: An analysis of its intellectual precedents and nature.* Unpublished dissertation, Green College, Oxford. (A variation of this study was published in 2002 by the Foundation for Educational Renewal.)

Ford, M. E. (1992). *Motivating humans: Goals, emotions, and personal agency beliefs.* Newbury Park, CA: Sage.

Franklin, J. (2005). Mental mileage. *ASCD Education Update, 47*(6), 1–4.

Fullan, M. (1997). Emotion and hope: Constructive concepts for complex times. In A. Hargreaves (Ed.), *Rethinking educational change with heart and mind: 1997 ASCD Yearbook* (pp. 216–223). Alexandria, VA: Association for Supervision and Curriculum Development.

Fullan, M. (2000, February). *Change forces: The sequel.* 2000 CHANGE Council Keynote Address presented at the annual meeting of the Association for Educational Communications and Technology, Long Beach, CA.

Fullan, M. (2001). *Leading in a culture of change.* San Francisco: Jossey-Bass.

Fullan, M., Bertani, A., & Quinn, J. (2004). New lessons for districtwide reform. *Educational Leadership, 61*(7), 42–46.

Gardner, H. (1995). *Intelligence: Multiple perspectives.* Fort Worth, TX: Harcourt Brace.

Gardner, H. (1999). *Intelligence reframed: Multiple intelligences for the 21st century.* New York: Basic Books.

Gay, G. (1995). *The nature of metacognition.* Retrieved September 6, 2005, from http://www.ldrc.ca/contents/view_article/146/

Glasser, W. (1984). *Control theory: A new explanation of how we control our lives.* New York: HarperCollins.

Glasser, W. (1990). *The quality school: Managing students without coercion.* New York: Harper Perennial.

Glasser, W. (1994). Foreword. In B. Greene (Ed.), *New paradigms for creating quality schools* (p. iv). Chapel Hill, NC: New View Publications.

Goals 2000: Educate America Act. (1994). Retrieved February 5, 2003, from http://www.neonrose.net/standardscourse/goals2000.html#

Gordon, E. W. (2004). Closing the gap: High achievement for students of color. *Research Points, 2*(3), 1–4.

Greenberg, M. T., Weissberg, R. P., O'Brien, M. U., Zins, J. E., Fredericks, L., Resnik, H., et al. (2003). Enhancing school-based prevention and youth development through coordinated social, emotional, and academic learning. *American Psychologist, 58*(6/7), 466–474.

Grossman, F. D., & Ancess, J. (2004). Narrowing the gap in affluent schools. *Educational Leadership, 62*(3), 70–73.

Haberman, M. (2004). Can star teachers create learning communities? *Educational Leadership, 61*(8), 52–56.

Hacker, D. J., Dunlosky, J., & Graesser, A. C. (1998). *Metacognition in educational theory and practice.* Hillsdale, NJ: Lawrence Erlbaum Associates.

Hannafin, M. (1999). *Learning in open-ended environments: Tools and technologies for the next millennium.* Available at http://tech1.coe.uga.edu/itforum/paper34/paper34.html

Hawley, W. D., & Valli, L. (2000). *Learner-centered professional development* [Research Bulletin No. 27]. Bloomington, IN: Phi Delta Kappa Center for Evaluation, Development, and Research.

Hay McBer. (2000, June). *Research into teacher effectiveness. Report to the UK Department for Education and Employment.* London: Author.

Hogan, E., & Kaiser, R. B. (2005). What we know about leadership. *Review of General Psychology, 9*(2), 169–180.

Holland, H. (2005). Teaching teachers: Professional development to improve student achievement. *Research Points, 3*(1), 1–2, 4.

Hoy, A. W. (2000). Educational psychology in teacher education. *Educational Psychologist, 35*(4), 257–270.

Jenkins, H. (2005). Getting into the game. *Educational Leadership, 62*(7), 48–51.

Jensen, E. (1998). *Teaching with the brain in mind.* Alexandria, VA: Association for Supervision and Curriculum Development.

Johnson, S. M., & Kardos, S. M. (2005). Bridging the generation gap. *Educational Leadership, 62*(8), 8–14.

Just for the Kids. (2003). *Promising practices: How high-performing schools in Texas get results.* Austin, TX: Author.

Kanfer, R., & McCombs, B. L. (2000). Motivation: Applying current theory to critical issues in training. In S. Tobias & D. T. Fletcher (Eds.), *Handbook of training* (pp. 85–108). New York: Macmillan.

Kantrowitz, B., & Springen, K. (2005, April 25). A peaceful adolescence. *Newsweek,* 58–61.

Keefe, J. W., & Jenkins, J. M. (2002). A special section on personalized instruction. *Phi Delta Kappan, 83*(6), 440–448.

Kelley, T. M., Mills, R. C., & Shuford, R. (2005). *A principle-based psychology of school violence prevention.*

Kenney, D. J., & Watson, T. S. (1998). *Crime in the schools: Reducing fear and disorder with student problem solving.* Washington, DC: Police Executive Research Forum.

Kofman, F., & Senge, P. M. (1993). Communities of commitment: The heart of learning organizations. *Organizational Dynamics, 22*(2), 5–24.

Kohn, A. (2005). Unconditional teaching. *Educational Leadership, 63*(1), 20–24.

Krajewski, B. (2005). In their own words. *Educational Leadership, 62*(6), 14–18.

Lambert, N., & McCombs, B. L. (Eds.). (1998). *How students learn: Reforming schools through learner-centered education.* Washington, DC: APA Books.

Larson, R. W. (2000). Toward a psychology of positive youth development. *American Psychologist, 55*(1), 170–183.

Lemke, J. L. (2002, April). *Complex systems and educational change.* Paper presented at the annual meeting of the American Educational Research Association, New Orleans.

Littky, D., Diaz, N., Dolly, D., Hempel, C., Plant, C., Price, P., et al. (2004). Moment to moment at the Met. *Educational Leadership, 61*(8), 39–43.

Livingston, J. A. (1997). *Metacognition: An overview.* Retrieved September 6, 2005, from http://www.gse.buffalo.edu/fas/ shuell/cep564/Metacog.htm

Marshall, H. H. (1992). *Redefining student learning: Roots of educational change.* Norwood, NJ: Ablex.

Marshall, H. H. (1996). Implications of differentiating and understanding constructivist approaches. *Educational Psychologist, 31*(3/4), 235–240.

Martin, R. A. (2002, April). *Alternatives in education: An exploration of learner-centered, progressive, and holistic education.* Paper presented at the annual meeting of the American Educational Research Association, New Orleans.

Mathews, J. (2004a, January 20). Turning strife into success. *Washington Post.* Retrieved January 22, 2004, from http:// www.washingtonpost.com/ac2/ wp-dyn/A31826-2004Jan20?language= printer

Mathews, J. (2004b, February 17). Seeking alternatives to standardized testing. *Washington Post.* Retrieved February 18, 2004, from http://www.washingtonpost.com/ac2/wp-dyn/A47699-2004Feb17? language=printer

McCombs, B. L. (1997). Self-assessment and reflection: Tools for promoting teacher changes toward learner-centered practices. *NASSP Bulletin, 81*(587), 1–14.

McCombs, B. L. (1998). Integrating metacognition, affect, and motivation in improving teacher education. In B. L. McCombs & N. Lambert (Eds.), *How students learn: Reforming schools through learner-centered education* (pp. 379–408). Washington, DC: APA Books.

McCombs, B. L. (1999a). *Violence prevention as a systemic, learner-centered approach: Building the connections necessary for positive growth and learning.* Unpublished concept paper. Denver, CO: University of Denver Research Institute.

McCombs, B. L. (1999b). What role does perceptual psychology play in educational reform today? In H. J. Freiberg (Ed.), *Perceiving, behaving, becoming: Lessons learned* (pp. 148–157). Alexandria, VA: Association for Supervision and Curriculum Development.

McCombs, B. (2000a, September). *Assessing the role of educational technology in the teaching and learning process: A learner-centered perspective.* Paper presented at the Secretary's Conference on Educational Technology: Measuring the Impacts and Shaping the Future, Washington, DC. Retrieved September 10, 2001, from http://www.ed.gov/rschstat/eval/ tech/techconf00/mccombs_paper.html

McCombs, B. L. (2000b). Reducing the achievement gap. *Society, 37*(5), 29–36.

McCombs, B. L. (2001). Self-regulated learning and academic achievement: A phenomenological view. In B. J. Zimmerman & D. H. Schunk (Eds.), *Self-regulated learning and academic achievement: Theoretical perspectives* (2nd ed., pp. 67–123). Mahwah, NJ: Erlbaum.

McCombs, B. L. (2003a). From credible research to policy for guiding educational reform. In W. M. Reynolds and G. E. Miller (Eds.), *Comprehensive handbook of psychology, volume 7: Educational psychology* (pp. 583–607). New York: Wiley.

McCombs, B. L. (2003b). Providing a framework for the redesign of K–12 education in the context of current educational reform issues. *Theory Into Practice, 42*(2), 93–101.

McCombs, B. L. (2004a). Learner-centered principles and practices: Enhancing motivation and achievement for children with learning challenges and disabilities. *International Review of Research in Mental Retardation, 28*, 85–120.

McCombs, B. L. (2004b). The learner-centered psychological principles: A framework for balancing a focus on academic achievement with a focus on social and emotional learning needs. In J. E. Zins, R. P. Weissberg, M. C. Wang, & H. J. Walberg (Eds.), *Building academic success on social and emotional learning: What does the research say?* (pp. 23–39). New York: Teachers College Press.

McCombs, B. L. (in press). Balancing accountability demands with research-validated, learner-centered teaching and learning practices. In C. E. Sleeter (Ed.), *Educating for democracy and equity in an era of accountability.* New York: Teachers College Press.

McCombs, B. L., & Bansberg, B. (1997). Meeting student diversity needs in poor, rural schools: Ideal practices and political realities. M. C. Wang & K. K. Wong (Eds.), *Implementing school reform: Practice and policy imperatives* (pp. 161–192). Philadelphia, PA: Temple University Center for Research in Human Development and Education.

McCombs, B. L., & Kanfer, R. (2000). Motivation. In H. F. O'Neil, Jr., & S. Tobias (Eds.), *Handbook on training* (pp. 85–108). New York: Macmillan.

McCombs, B. L., & Lauer, P. A. (1997). Development and validation of the learner-centered battery: Self-assessment tools for teacher reflection and professional development. *The Professional Educator, 20*(1), 1–21.

McCombs, B. L., & Lauer, P. A. (1998, July). *The learner-centered model of seamless professional development: Implications for practice and policy changes in higher education.* Paper presented at the 23rd International Conference on Improving University Teaching, Dublin.

McCombs, B. L., Perry, K. E., & Daniels, D. H. (in press). Understanding children's and teachers' perceptions of learner centered practices: Implications for early schooling. *Elementary School Journal.*

McCombs, B. L., & Quiat, M. A. (2002). What makes a comprehensive school reform model learner-centered? *Urban Education, 37*(4), 476–496.

McCombs, B. L., & Vakili, D. (2005). A learner-centered framework for e-learning. *Teachers College Record, 107*(8), 1582–1600.

McCombs, B. L., & Whisler, J. S. (1997). *The learner-centered classroom and school: Strategies for increasing student motivation and achievement.* San Francisco: Jossey-Bass.

McLuhan, M. (1989). *The global village: Transformations in world life and media in the 21st century.* New York: Oxford University Press.

McNabb, M. L., & McCombs, B. K. (2001). *Designs for e-learning: A vision and emerging framework.* Paper prepared for the PT3 Vision Quest on Assessment in e-Learning Cultures. Available at www.pt3.org

Meece, J. L. (2002). *Child and adolescent development for educators* (2nd ed.). New York: McGraw-Hill.

Meece, J. L., Herman, P., & McCombs, B. L. (2003). Relations of learner-centered teaching practices to adolescents' achievement goals. *International Journal of Educational Research, 39*(4–5), 457–475.

Meier, D. (2002). Standardization versus standards. *Phi Delta Kappan, 84*(3), 190–198.

Miller, S., Duffy, G. G., Rohr, J., Gasparello, R., & Mercier, S. (2005). Preparing teachers for high-poverty schools. *Educational Leadership, 62*(8), 62–65.

Mitra, D. L. (2002, April). *Makin' it real: Involving youth in school reform.* Paper presented in the International Symposium on "Student Voices and Democracy in Schools" at the annual meeting of the American Educational Research Association, New Orleans.

Moon, T. R., Callahan, C. M., & Tomlinson, C. A. (2003, April 28). Effects of state testing programs on elementary schools with high concentrations of student poverty—Good news or bad news? *Current Issues in Education, 6*(8), 1–3.

Murray, C., & Malmgren, K. (2005). Implementing a teacher-student relationship in a high-poverty urban school: Effects on social, emotional, and academic adjustment and lessons learned. *Journal of School Psychology, 43,* 137–152.

Nation, M., Crusto, C., Wandersman, A., Kumpfer, K. L., Seyolt, D., Morrissey-Kane, E., et al. (2003). What works in prevention: Principles of effective prevention programs. *American Psychologist, 58*(6/7), 449–456.

The National Commission on Excellence in Education. (1983, April). *Nation at risk: The imperative for educational reform.* Washington, DC: U.S. Department of Education. Available online at http://www.neonrose.net/standards course/wherebegan.html#

National Public Radio. (2005, March 21). *Testing scandal in Texas schools.* Retrieved September 12, 2005, from http://www.npr.org/templates/ story/story.php?storyId=4544036

National Study Group for the Affirmative Development of Academic Ability. (2004). *All students reaching the top: Strategies for closing academic achievement gaps.* Naperville, IL: Learning Point.

Neill, M. (2003). The dangers of testing. *Educational Leadership, 60*(5), 43–46.

Noddings, N. (2005). What does it mean to educate the whole child? *Educational Leadership, 63*(1), 8–13.

Osher, D., & Fleischman, S. (2005). Research matters: Positive culture in urban schools. *Educational Leadership, 62*(6), 84–85.

Palmer, P. J. (1998). *The courage to teach: Exploring the inner landscape of a teacher's life.* San Francisco: Jossey-Bass.

Palmer, P. J. (1999). Evoking the spirit in public education. *Educational Leadership, 56*(4), 6–11.

Patterson, W. (2003). Breaking out of our boxes. *Phi Delta Kappan, 84*(8), 569–574.

Perkins-Gough, D. (2005). Fixing high schools. *Educational Leadership, 62*(70), 88–89.

Perry, K. E., & Daniels, D. H. (2004, April). *Elementary students' perceptions of teachers and school adjustment.* Paper presented as part of the interactive symposium The Case for Learner-Centered Practices Across the K–12 and College Levels at the annual meeting of American Educational Research Association, San Diego.

Perry, K. E., & Weinstein, R. S. (1998). The social context of early schooling and children's school adjustment. *Educational Psychologist, 33*(4), 177–194.

Phillips, M. (1997). What makes schools effective? A comparison of the relationships of communitarian climate and academic climate to mathematics achievement and attendance during middle school. *American Educational Research Journal, 34,* 543–578.

Pierce, J. W., Holt, J. K., Kolar, C., & McCombs, B. L. (2004, April). *Testing the learner-centered model with data at the college level.* Paper presented as part of the interactive symposium The Case for Learner-Centered Practices Across the K–12 and College Levels at the annual meeting of American Educational Research Association, San Diego.

Polloway, E., Miller, L., & Smith, T. E. C. (2004). *Language instruction for students with disabilities* (3rd ed.). Denver, CO: Love.

Price, L. F. (2005). The biology of risk taking. *Educational Leadership, 62*(7), 22–26.

Putnam, R. T., & Borko, H. (2000). What do new views of knowledge and thinking have to say about research on teacher learning? *Educational Researcher, 29*(1), 4–15.

Renzulli, J. S., & Reis, S. M. (1985). *The schoolwide enrichment model: A comprehensive plan for educational excellence.* Mansfield Center, CT: Creative Learning Press.

Renzulli, J. S., Reis, S. M., Hebert, T. P., & Diaz, E. I. (1995). The plight of high-ability students in urban schools. In M. C. Wang & M. C. Reynolds (Eds.), *Making a difference for students at risk* (pp. 61–98). Thousand Oaks, CA: Corwin Press.

Rodriguez, E. R. (2005, April). *Using creative, enriched instruction to advance African American students' achievement.* Presentation at the annual meeting of the Association for Supervision and Curriculum Development, Orlando.

Rogers, C., & Freiberg, H. J. (1994). *Freedom to learn* (3rd ed.). New York: Merrill.

Rubalcava, M. (2005). Let kids come first. *Educational Leadership, 62*(8), 70–72.

Rudduck, J., Day, J., & Wallace, G. (1997). Student perspectives on school improvement. In A. Hargreaves (Ed.), *1997 ASCD Yearbook: Rethinking educational change with heart and mind* (pp. 73–91). Alexandria, VA: Association for Supervision and Curriculum Development.

Russell, A. (2004, August 2). Pillars of wisdom. *The Age.* Retrieved August 2, 2004, from http://www.theage.com.au/ articles/2004

Ryan, A. M., & Patrick, H. (2001). The classroom social environment and changes in adolescents' motivation and engagement during middle school. *American Educational Research Journal, 38*(2), 437–460.

Ryan, R. M., & Deci, E. L. (2000). Self-determination theory and the facilitation of intrinsic motivation, social development, and well-being. *American Psychologist, 55*(1), 68–78.

Sanders, W. L., & Rivers, J. C. (1996). *Cumulative and residual effects of teachers on future student academic achievement.* Knoxville, TN: University of Tennessee Value-Added Research and Assessment Center.

Satcher, D. (2005, April). *The obesity epidemic: What is it costing schools?* Presentation at the annual meeting of the Association for Supervision and Curriculum Development, Orlando.

Sato, M. (2000, April). *The National Board for Professional Teaching Standards: Teacher learning through the assessment process.* Paper presented at the Annual Meeting of the American Educational Research Association, New Orleans.

Schaps, E., & Lewis, C. (1999). Perils on an essential journey: Building school community. *Phi Delta Kappan, 81*(3), 215–218.

Schuh, K. L., Wade, P. A., & Knupp, T. L. (2005, April). *Intellectually useful personal connections: Linking what students know with what they learn.* Paper presented at the annual meeting of the American Educational Research Association, Montreal, Quebec.

Seligman, M. E. P., & Csikszentmihalyi, M. (2000). Positive psychology: An introduction. *American Psychologist, 55*(1), 5–14.

Senge, P. M. (1990). *The fifth discipline: The art and practice of the learning organization.* New York: Doubleday.

Sergiovanni, T. J. (2004). Building a community of hope. *Educational Leadership, 61*(8), 33–37.

Shechtman, S. (2005). *Empowering the classroom teacher as advocate and policy informant.* Presentation at the annual meeting of the Association for Supervision and Curriculum Development, Orlando.

Shepard, L. A. (2000). The role of assessment in a learning culture. *Educational Researcher, 29*(7), 4–14.

Shulman, L. (2001). Understanding teachers and their learning. *New Educator,* 1–5.

Sparks, D., & Hirsh, S. (1997). *A new vision for staff development.* Alexandria, VA: Association for Supervision and Curriculum Development.

Special report: Early exit—Denver's graduation gap. (2005, May 16–20). *Rocky Mountain News,* pp. 1S–12S.

Sroka, S. (2005, April). *Empowering students.* Presentation at the annual meeting of the Association for Supervision and Curriculum Development, Orlando.

Summers, J. J., Beretvas, S. N., Svinicki, M. D., & Gorin, J. S. (2005). Evaluating collaborative learning and community. *Journal of Experimental Education, 73*(3), 165–188.

Sylwester, R. (1995). *A celebration of neurons: An educator's guide to the brain.* Alexandria, VA: Association for Supervision and Curriculum Development.

Taylor, K. L. (2003). Through the eyes of students. *Educational Leadership, 60*(4), 72–75.

Tomlinson, C. A., & Doubet, K. (2005). Reach them to teach them. *Educational Leadership, 62*(7), 9–15.

Tomlinson, J. (1999). *Globalization and culture.* Chicago: University of Chicago Press.

Tompkins, J. (1990, October). Pedagogy of the distressed. *College English, 52*(6), 653–660.

Valencia, R. R., Valenzuela, A., Sloan, K., & Foley, D. E. (2001). Let's treat the cause, not the symptoms: Equity and accountability in Texas revisited. *Phi Delta Kappan, 83*(4), 318–326.

Vaughn, A. L. (2005). The self-paced student. *Educational Leadership, 62*(7), 69–73.

Wagner, T. (2003). Reinventing America's schools. *Phi Delta Kappan, 84*(9), 665–668.

Wandersman, A., & Florin, P. (2003). Community interventions and effective prevention. *American Psychologist, 58*(6/7), 441–448.

Weinberger, E., & McCombs, B. L. (2003). Applying the LCPs to high school education. *Theory Into Practice, 42*(2), 117–126.

Weinstein, R. S. (1998). Promoting positive expectations in schooling. In N. Lambert & B. L. McCombs (Eds.), *How students learn: Reforming schools through learner-centered education.* New York: APA Books.

Weissberg, R. P., Kumpfer, K. L., & Seligman, M. E. P. (2003). Prevention that works for children and youth. *American Psychologist, 58*(6/7), 425–432.

Welsh, P. (2004, May 3). Perfect—and hard to reach. *Washington Post.* Retrieved May 3, 2003, from http://www.washingtonpost.com

Wheatley, M. J. (1999a). *Leadership and the new science: Discovering order in a chaotic world* (2nd ed.). San Francisco: Berrett-Koehler.

Wheatley, M. J. (1999b, July). *Reclaiming hope: The new story is ours to tell.* Salt Lake City: Summer Institute, University of Utah.

Wheatley, M. J., & Kellner-Rogers, M. (1998, April-May). Bringing life to organizational change. *Journal of Strategic Performance Measurement,* 5–13.

White House Initiative on Educational Excellence for Hispanic Americans. (1999). *What works for Latino youth* (2nd ed.). Washington, DC: U.S. Department of Education.

Williams, B. (2003). *Closing the achievement gap: A vision for changing beliefs and practices* (2nd ed.). Alexandria, VA: Association for Supervision and Curriculum Development.

Williams, B. (2005, April). *Improving achievement for students in poverty: A forum.* Presentation at the annual meeting of the Association for Supervision and Curriculum Development, Orlando.

Wlodkowski, R. J., & Ginsberg, M. B. (1995). *Diversity and motivation: Culturally responsive teaching.* San Francisco: Jossey-Bass.

Wolfe, P., & Sorgen, M. (1990). *Mind, memory, and learning.* Napa, CA: Author.

Wolk, R. A. (2005, May 1). Perspective: The silent majority. *Teacher Magazine.* Retrieved June 12, 2005, from http://www.edweek.org/tm/articles/2005/05/01

Yee, D. (2004, July 20). Violence scares kids into avoiding school. *Des Moines Register.* Retrieved July 30, 2004, from http://hosted.ap.org/dynamic/stories/S/SCHOOL_VIOLENCE?

Zimmerman, B. J., & Schunk, D. H. (Eds.). (2001). *Self-regulated learning and academic achievement: Theoretical perspectives* (2nd ed.). Mahwah, NJ: Erlbaum.

Zins, J. E., Elias, M. J., Greenberg, M. T., & Weissberg, R. P. (2000). Promoting social and emotional competence in children. In K. M. Minke & G. G. Bear (Eds.), *Preventing school problems—promoting school success: Strategies and programs that work* (pp. 71–99). Bethesda, MD: National Association of School Psychologists.

Zurawsky, C. (2004). Teachers matter: Evidence from value-added assessments. *Research Points, 2*(2), 1–2, 4.

Index

Absenteeism, 17
Accountability, x, 34–35, 133, 139
  standards and, 34, 72
Achievement gaps, 79–81, 85, 91
Achievements, x, xi, 17, 23, 145
  accountability/standards and, 34
  ALCP surveys and, 117
  caring teachers and, 73
  change and, 112
  control/choice and, 16
  individual differences and, 60
  international schools and, 41
  low-income and, 64
  reform and, 38
  strategies for creating learner-
    centered classrooms and, 97
  student/teacher relationships and, 58.
    See also Relationships
  student voice and, 96–97
  students as partners and, 112–113
Affective factors, 22, 23 (Figure), 30–31,
  32, 45, 46 (Figure)
  motivation and, 52–55
African Americans, 81, 85
  See also Minorities
Alexander, P. A., 32n 1
Alienation, x, 6, 7, 19, 23, 34, 36
Alvarez, H. K., 94
America 2000, 34
American Educational Research
  Association (AERA), 81
American Psychological Association
  (APA), xi, 24–25, 34, 35, 45, 47
Amrein, A. L., 35
Ancess, J., 79, 81
Anxiety, 52–53, 58
APA Task Force, 34, 158
APA Work Group of the Board of
  Educational Affairs, 25, 35

Assessment of Learner-Centered
  Practices (ALCP), 24, 25, 117–120,
  118–119 (Figure), 139, 141
  examples of, 122 (Figure),
    124–125 (Figure)
  feedback and, 121, 140
  strategies for determining professional
    development needs and, 128
  teacher beliefs surveys and, 26–29,
    130, 132
  understanding sample feedback
    and, 123
Assessments, 62–63
  academic outcomes and, 72
ALCP surveys and, 117
  diversity and, 32
  feedback and, 35, 50
  personal domain and, 19
At-risk youth, 96
Attendance, 108 (Figure), 112–113

Battistich, V., 36
Behavior:
  disruptive, 88
  high-risk, 64
Beliefs, 129, 135
  ALCP example and, 122 (Figure)
  caring teachers and, 74, 122 (Figure)
  diversity and, 60
  educators and, 71
  living systems and, 21, 22 (Figure)
  motivation and, 52
  nature of the learning process
    and, 47
  policies and, 114
  reflections and, 142
  supporting teachers and, 140
  surveys and, 115, 117, 118 (Figure),
    119 (Figure), 130–131

Belonging, 36, 57, 97, 100 (Figure)
Berliner, D. C., 35, 64
Biglan, A., 64, 95
Blum, R. W., 90, 91
Boredom, 48, 97
Borko, H., 16
Borman, G. D., 6
Bracey, G. W., 74, 75
Brain functions, 32n 1, 37, 46–47
Bransford, J. D., 37, 46, 47, 49, 52
Brehm, K., 93
Brown, A. L., 37, 46
Bruner, J., xi
Bullying, 80, 94

Cacioppo, J. T., 56
Caine, G., 37
Caine, R. N., 37
Callahan, C. M., 63
Calvert, M., 40
Carey, K., 79, 85
Carnine, D., 95
Carter, G. R., 94
Centeredness, 25, 121
Challenges:
    ALCP surveys and, 119 (Figure)
    non-negotiables and, 102
    students and, 91–92
    test scores and, 62
Change, ix, 17, 32, 157, 159
    achievements and, 112
    becoming a magnet for, 126–128
    classrooms and, 101
    decision making and, 40
    international schools and, 41
    living systems and, 21–22
    managing resistance to, 136–142
    policies and, 115
    stages of personal, 137 (Figure)
    support and, 138–142
    teachers and, 24, 106–107
Choice, 4–5, 25
    ALCP surveys and, 118 (Figure)
    change and, 136
    children and, 38
    classroom management and, 96
    effective LCPs for students in grades
        4–12 and, 92
    intrinsic motivation and, 53–54
    non-negotiables and, 101

responsibilities and, 112
self-motivated learning and, 16
strategies for creating learner-centered
    classrooms and, 100 (Figure)
students and, 8, 38
Classrooms:
    climate and, 75–78, 87, 88, 112
    context of learning and, 51
    management and, 86, 93–96, 104
    plans for, 135–136
    relationships and, 67, 73. *See also*
        Relationships
    size and, 91
    strategies for creating learner-centered
        and, 96–101, 99–100 (Figure)
Cleland, J., 153
Coaching, 140
Coalition of Self-Learning, 135
Cocking, R. R., 37, 46
Cognitive factors, xi, 17, 22,
        23 (Figure), 30 (Table)
    domains and, 45, 46–52, 46 (Figure)
    social influences on learning and, 57
Collins, V., 61, 80
Combs, A. W., 32n 1, 37, 72
Comer, J. P., 97
Common sense, 96
Communications, 141
    adults/children and, 56
    policies and, 115
    social influences on learning
        and, 57
    students/teachers and, 39, 40
Competence, 36, 53–54, 105
Comprehension, 54
Control, 4–5, 25, 36
    ALCP surveys and, 118 (Figure)
    classroom management and,
        86, 93–96, 104
    effective LCPs for students in grades
        4–12 and, 92
    home schooling and, 135
    intrinsic motivation and, 53–54
    non-negotiables and, 104
    relationships and, 25
    responsibilities and, 112, 113
    school leaders and, 38
    self-motivated learning and, 16
    sharing, 9
    students and, 24

Cook-Sather, A., 41
Corbett, D., 73, 74
Crabtree, S., 91
Critical thinking, 5–6, 18, 133
    cognitive functions and, 47
    quality school work and, 74
    schools established for, 72
    surveys and, 115
    systems and, 18
    testing and, 35
    young children and, 37
    See also Metacognitive factors;
        Reflective thinking; Thinking
Csikszentmihalyi, M., 25
Culture, 79, 157
    context of learning and, 51
    developmental influence
        and, 56
    diversity and, 60
    effective LCPs for students in grades
        4–12 and, 91
    promoting a positive, 62
    strategies for creating learner-centered
        classrooms and, 97
    teacher's recognition of, 33
Curiosity, 36, 52, 53, 79, 119 (Figure)
Curriculum:
    achievement gaps and, 64, 80
    balancing academic/nonacademic,
        63–64
    challenge and, 41
    classroom climate and, 77
    ideal high schools and, 98
    personal domain and, 19
    quality school work and, 74
    reflections and, 51
    social environments and, 81
    standards and, 62
    student forums and, 39
    students and, 8
    time and, 63

Daniels, D. H., 58, 87, 89, 98
Darling-Hammond, L., 16, 74
Davis, H. A., 58
Day, J., 37, 41, 58
Deci, E. L., 6, 36, 53
Decision making, 6
    ideal high schools and, 98
    involving students in, 40

LCPs and, 16, 22–23, 23 (Figure)
    learning and, 7, 40
    personal domains and, 19
    school leaders and, 38
    student voice and, 96
Developmental factors, xi, 8, 22, 23,
        31, 32, 55–58
    domains and, 45, 46 (Figure)
    teacher's recognition of, 33
Developmental psychologists, 47, 92
Dewey, J., xi, 72
Dialogue. *See* Communications
Diamond, M., 37, 63
Diet, 64, 80
Dillon, S., 93
Disabilities, 56
Discipline problems, 96
Diversity, 6–7, 19, 24, 25, 31, 32, 77
Doll, B., 93, 96
Doubet, K., 78
Dropouts, 6
    effective LCPs for students in grades
        4–12 and, 91
    factual recall and, 97
    quality school work and, 74
    standards and, 17, 72–73
    testing and, 35
Drug abuse, 75, 80, 85, 95
DuFour, R., 38
Dunlosky, J., 47

Educational reform, x
Effective Lifelong Learning Inventory
    (ELLI), 153
Eisner, E., 72
Ellet, F. S., Jr., 38
Emotional factors, xi, 6, 8, 20, 23, 30–31,
        32, 52–53
    domains and, 45, 46 (Figure)
    effective LCPs for students in grades
        4–12 and, 91
    health and, 133
    strategies for creating learner-centered
        classrooms and, 98 (Figure)
    student outcomes and, 108 (Figure)
    teacher's recognition of, 33
    testing and, 35
Environmental factors:
    classroom climate and, 76
    context of learning and, 51

effective LCPs for students in grades
    4–12 and, 91
    individual differences and, 59
    quality school work and, 74, 75
Ericson, D. P., 38
Espinoza, S., 153

Fabes, R., 56, 92
Faith, 20
Families, 64
    change and, 107
    classroom climate and, 77
    classroom management and,
        93, 94, 95
    diversity and, 62
    individual differences factors
        and, 93
    involvement and, 65
    policies and, 113–114, 115
    social influences on learning and, 57
    standards and, 72
Fear, ix–x, 52, 53, 54, 107
Feistritzer, C. E., 16
Ferrero, D. J., 71, 145
Field trips, 142
Fielding, M., 41
Flay, B. R., 95
Fleischman, S., 62, 64, 91
Flock, L., 64, 91
Florin, P., 65, 94
Foley, D. E., 85
Forbes, S., 6
Ford, M. E., 32n 1
Forums, 39–40
Franklin, J., 92
Freiberg, H. J., 37, 38, 44, 147, 148
Fullan, M., 17, 21, 120, 140
Funding, 40

Gardner, H., 60
Gay, G., 46
Ginsberg, M. B., 157
Glasser, W., 36, 38, 67, 74, 75
Goals 2000: Educate America Act, 34
Gordon, E. W., 62, 64, 79, 91
Graesser, A. C., 47
Greenberg, M. T., 65, 95
Grossman, F. D., 79, 81
Guided Reflection and Feedback
    Process, 121, 123

Hacker, D. J., 47
Hannafin, M., 5
Harper, D., 154
Hawkley, L. C., 56
Hay McBer report, 78
Health issues, 64
    achievement gaps and, 80, 81
    classroom management and, 94
    strategies for creating learner-
        centered classrooms and, 97
    See also Mental health
Heredity, 59
Herman, P., 55, 89
Hirsh, S., 16, 18
Hispanics, 85, 97–98
    See also Minorities
Holt, J. K., 58, 89
Home schooling, 6, 135
Hope, 20, 37, 136, 137 (Figure)
Hopson, J., 37

Individual differences factors, xi, 22, 23,
    25, 31, 32, 35, 46 (Figure), 60
    developmental influence on learning
        and, 56–57
    domains/factors influencing learners
        and, 45
    effective LCPs for students in grades
        4–12 and, 89, 93
    teacher's recognition of, 33, 34
Inquiry-based learning, 55
Intervention programs, 65
Isolation, 18, 25, 36
    See also Alienation

Jenkins, H., 91, 92
Jenkins, J. M., 8
Jensen, E., 37
Johnson's Awareness Quotient, 150–152
Journals, 42, 136, 142
    beliefs/values and, 71
    classroom climate and, 76
    effects of motivation on effort to
        learn and, 55
    quality teachers and, 78
    reflections and, 9
Just for the Kids, 97

Kalkman, D. L., 87
Kanfer, R., 32, 32n 1

Keefe, J. W., 8
Kelley, T. M., 65, 96
Kellner-Rogers, M., 17, 19
Kenney, D. J., 38
Knowledge, 5–6, 16
   assessment and, 62
   change and, 137 (Figure)
   classroom climate and, 76
   classroom management and, 96
   construction of, 49
   decision making and, 7
   effects of motivation on efforts to
      learn and, 54
   games and, 91–92
   goals of the learning process and, 47
   linear teaching of, 25
   personalized learning and, 8
   student outcomes and, 107–108
   teaching and, 23
Knupp, T. L., 92
Kohn, A., 72, 73, 141
Kolar, C., 58, 89
Kumpfer, K. L., 94

Lambert, N., 32n 1, 41, 47, 48, 51, 52
Larson, R. W., 25
Latinos, 85, 97–98
   See also Minorities
Lauer, P. A., 24, 25
Leadership:
   change and, 126, 137 (Figure)
   classroom management and, 95
   living systems and, 20
   teachers and, 7
Leadership teams, 141
Learner-Centered Model (LCM), 9, 17,
   21–24, 32, 45
Learner-Centered Rubric (LCR),
   117, 127, 145
Learning, ix–x
   change and, 136. See also Change
   developmental influences on, 56–57
   diversity and, 60–62
   effective LCPs for students in grades
      4–12 and, 89–90
   effective LCPs for students in K–3
      and, 87, 88 (Figure)
   individual differences in, 59–60
   natural lifelong process and, 35–36
   social factors on, 57–59

   supporting teachers and, 140–141
   teachers and, 7–9, 20, 32, 40, 113
   who's in charge of student's, 107–112
   who's in charge of teacher's, 105–107
Lemke, J. L., 17
Living systems, 9, 17, 18, 19–20,
      19 (Figure), 158
   change and, 21, 137, 138, 159
   elements of, 22 (Figure)
Livingston, J. A., 46, 47
Low-achieving students, 35, 62–63, 85
Low-income, 60
   achievement gaps and, 64, 79–80
   classroom climate and, 76
   testing and, 35

Malmgren, K., 64, 91
Management, 86, 93–96, 104
Marshall, H. H., 32n 1
Martin, C. L., 6, 56, 92
Martin, R. A., 6
Masi, C. M., 56
Math, 6, 50, 58, 76, 81, 89
Mathews, J., 97
McBer, H., 76, 77, 78
McCombs, B. L.:
   achievements/motivation and, 87
   anxiety/fear and, 53
   choice/control and, 54
   classroom climate and, 75
   classroom management and, 94
   context of learning and, 52
   developmental and social factors
      and, 55
   distinguishing learner-centered
      teachers and, 88
   ecology of learning and, 17–18
   effective LCPs for students in grades
      4–12 and, 89, 90, 91
   effective teaching and, 37
   efforts to learn and, 55
   environments and, 36
   goals and, 48
   healthy classrooms and, 67
   home schooling and, 135
   individualizing and, 59
   LCM and, 24
   learner-centeredness and, 16, 25,
      69, 120
   managing change and, 136

math class story and, 65, 66–67
metacognition factors and, 47
modeling and, 50
natural learning and, 4
promoting motivation/achievements
    and, 15
quality school work and, 75
relationships and, 25, 41, 58
sharing control/power and, 9
student outcomes and, 107
teacher beliefs survey and, 132
technical and organizational
    changes and, 19
technology-supported networked
    learning communities and, 32
thinking about thinking and, 51
violence preventions and, 80
McLuhan, M., 5
Meaning, 22, 45–46, 47
Medical care, 64
Meece, J. L., 55, 56, 58, 89, 92
Meier, D., 97
Memorization, 5, 46, 47, 48
Mental health, 64
  classroom management and,
      94, 96
  LCPs and, 35
  standards and, 72–73
  violence and, 65, 96
  See also Health issues
Mentkowski, M., 153
Mentoring:
  achievement gaps and, 81
  ALCP surveys and, 117
  change and, 136–137
  strategies for creating learner-centered
      classrooms and, 97
  students as, 93
  support and, 139, 140
  teachers and, 64
Metacognitive factors, xi, 22,
      23 (Figure), 30 (Table)
  domains and, 45, 46–52, 46 (Figure)
  effective LCPs for students in grades
      4–12 and, 92
  thinking about thinking and,
      30 (Table), 46 (Figure), 47, 50–51
  See also Critical thinking
Miller, L., 43, 68, 69, 92, 135
Mills, R. C., 65, 96

Minorities:
  achievement gaps and, 79–80, 81
  African Americans, 81, 85
  classroom climate and, 76
  diversity and, 60
  dropouts and, 97
  Hispanics, 85, 97–98
  individual differences and, 60
  success and, 6
Miser, A. B., 32n 1
Mitra, D. L., 38, 39, 97
Modeling, 81, 98, 136–137
Montessori schools, 6
Moon, T. R., 63
Morale achievements, 8
Motivational factors, 19, 20, 22,
      24, 25, 30–31
  ALCP surveys and,
      117, 119 (Figure)
  classroom management and, 96
  context of learning and, 51
  curiosity and, 53
  diversity and, 60–61
  domains/factors influencing learners
      and, 45, 46 (Figure)
  effective LCPs for students in grades
      4–12 and, 89
  effects of motivation on effort to
      learn and, 54–55
  intrinsic, 18, 30, 35, 54, 105, 158
  LCPs and, 23
  non-negotiables and, 105
  policies and, 113–114
  reform and, 38
  strategies for creating learner-centered
      classrooms and, 97
  stress and, 98
Mrazek, P. J., 95
Murphy, P. K., 32, 32n 1
Murray, C., 64, 91

Name tags, 43, 44, 147
Nation, M., 65, 95
Nation at Risk report, 34
National Assessment of Educational
    Progress (NAEP), 35
National Commission on Excellence in
    Education, 34
National Education Goals, 34
National Governors' Association, 34

National Public Radio, 62
National Study Group for the
    Affirmative Development of
    Academic Ability, 60, 76
Negativity, 17, 23, 107
    change and, 107
    curiosity and, 54
    dropouts and, X
    motivation and, 52–53, 54, 72
    peer pressure and, 80
    social influences and, 58
    whole child and, 72
Neill, M., 35
No Child Left Behind (NCLB), 85
Noddings, N., 58, 72
Non-English-speaking students, 35
Nutrition, 64, 80

Ollendick, T. H., 94
Osher, D., 62, 64, 91
Overman, L. T., 5, 6

Palmer, P. J., 8
Parental involvement, 38
    achievement gaps and, 81, 85
    change and, 139
    developmental influence and, 56
    effective partners and, 20
    quality school work and, 75
    strategies for creating learner-centered
        classrooms and, 98 (Figure)
Patterson, W., 74
Peers, 55, 56
    academic performance and, 64, 91
    achievement gaps and, 80
    strategies for creating learner-centered
        classrooms and, 101
    support and, 139
Perry, K. E., 32n 1, 58, 87, 89
Personal domain, 19
Personal factors, 113–114
Phillips, M., 6
Physical education, 135
Pierce, J. W., 58, 89
Policies, 113–115, 142
    living systems and, 20, 22 (Figure)
    student forums and, 40
Polloway, E., 92
Poverty. See Low-income
Power sharing, 112

Practice implications, 112–115
Prevention, 64, 65
Problem solving:
    classroom climate and, 76
    individual differences and, 60
    quality school work and, 74
    social influences on learning and, 58
    strategic thinking and, 49–50
    strategies for creating learner-centered
        classrooms and, 100 (Figure)
Putnam, R. T., 16

Quiat, M. A., 37

Reflective thinking, 16, 142
    ALCP surveys and, 118 (Figure)
    curriculum and, 51
    journals and, 9
    personalized learning and, 8
    policies and, 115
    social influences on learning and, 57
    summary of, 144–145
    teacher retention and, 113
    time and, 8
    See also Critical thinking; Thinking
Relationships, 9, 17, 18
    academic performance and, 64
    achievement gaps and, 80, 81
    ALCP surveys and, 118–119 (Figure)
    caring teachers and, 73, 80,
        81, 98, 112, 118 (Figure),
        122 (Figure), 140
    change and, 22, 138
    classrooms and, 67, 76, 77, 94, 95, 96
    control and, 25
    developmental influence and, 57
    effective LCPs for students in grades
        4–12 and, 89, 90 (Figure), 91
    effective LCPs for students in K–3
        and, 87, 88 (Figure)
    importance of, 61–62
    individual differences and, 58–59, 60
    intrinsic motivation and, 54
    LCPs and, 23
    non-negotiables and, 105
    policies and, 115
    reform efforts and, 19
    strategies for creating learner-centered
        classrooms and, 98 (Figure)
    student outcomes and, 110, 111

students/teachers and, 6, 8, 32, 36, 39, 40, 58
support and, 36, 139
Remembering, 5, 46, 47, 48
Repetti, R., 91
Respect:
    effective LCPs for students in grades 4–12 and, 91
    non-negotiables and, 104–105
    policies and, 114–115
    social influences on learning and, 59
    strategies for creating learner-centered classrooms and, 98 (Figure), 100 (Figure)
    student/teacher relationships and, 58
    students and, 37, 38
Responsibility, 5
    caring teachers and, 74, 80, 81, 98, 112, 118 (Figure), 122 (Figure), 140
    children and, 38
    choice/control and, 112, 113
    collective, 8
    effective LCPs for students in grades 4–12 and, 91, 92
    learning and, 7
    nature of the learning process and, 47
    non-negotiables and, 101–102
    ownership and, 112
    social influences on learning and, 59
    strategies for creating learner-centered classrooms and, 100 (Figure)
    students and, 20, 25, 32, 38
    support and, 139
    thinking about thinking and, 50–51
Retention, teacher, 6, 34, 35, 113
Reward systems, 141
Rickett, E. M., 56
Rivers, J. C., 37
Rodriguez, E. R., 61, 80
Rogers, C., 37, 38
Rote memorization, 5, 46, 47, 48
Rubalcava, M., 133, 135
Rubrics, 100 (Figure), 101, 114, 117, 129, 132
Rudduck, J., 41, 58
Russell, A., 63
Ryan, R. M., 6, 36, 53

Safety, 76, 89–90, 91, 98
Sanders, W. L., 37

Satcher, D., 80
Sato, M., 37
Schaps, E., 36
Scheduling, 40
Schools:
    alternative, 6, 135
    established for moral and social reasons, 72
    high-stakes testing and, 35. *See also* Testing
    international reform and, 41–42
    LCPs and, 25
    living systems and, 19–20
    reform and, 40
    responsibilities and, 113
    vision for, 129, 133, 135
Schuh, K. L., 92
Schunk, D. H., 4, 47
Schwab, J., xi
Self-awareness, 8, 122 (Figure)
Self-control, 96
Self-esteem, 6, 57, 65, 94, 96, 135
Self-reflections *See* Reflective thinking
Self-regulation, 47, 89, 92, 119 (Figure)
Seligman, M. E. P., 25, 94
Sergiovanni, T. J., 20
Shechtman, S., 81
Shuford, R., 65, 96
Sloan, K., 85
Smith, T. E. C., 92
Social factors, 5, 6, 17, 22, 23, 31, 32
    achievement gaps and, 64, 81
    alternative schools and, 6, 135
    context of learning and, 51
    domains/factors influencing learners and, 45, 46 (Figure)
    effective LCPs for students in grades 4–12 and, 91
    justice and, 6
    learning and, 57–59
    standards and, 17
    strategies for creating learner-centered classrooms and, 100 (Figure)
    student outcomes and, 108 (Figure)
    teachers design experiences for, 72
    teacher's recognition of, 33
Soloman, D., 36
Sorgen, M., 37
Sparks, D., 16, 18

Special report: Early exit—Denver's
      graduation gap, 97
Spirituality, 55–56
Sroka, S., 80
Standards, x, 6, 62–63
   academic achievements and, 17, 34
   cannot take precedence over
         individual learners, 112
   diversity and, 32
   knowledge and, 5
   NAEP and, 35
   neglect social and emotional
         qualities, 72
   personal domain and, 19
   quality school work and, 74
   See also Testing
Strategic thinking, 49–50
See also Critical thinking
Stress, 81, 98, 144
   standards and, 72–73
   testing and, 98
Student achievements
      See Achievements
Student forums, 39–40
Student voices, 9, 32, 36, 37
   effective LCPs for students in grades
         4–12 and, 89, 90 (Figure)
   strategies for honoring, 38–40
   See also Voice
Summer programs, 64
Support groups, 141
Surveys, 24, 126, 128, 129
   administrators and parents and, 139
   how to use, 135–136
   learner-centered and, 115–121, 116
         (Figure), 118–119 (Figure)
   teacher beliefs and,
         130–131 (Figure), 132
Sylwester, R., 37
Systems thinking, 18
   See also Critical thinking

Taylor, K. L., 79, 81, 85
Teachers:
   above average, 85
   caring and, 73, 80, 81, 98, 112,
         118 (Figure), 122 (Figure), 140
   evaluations and, 115–116
   ideal, 78
   leadership and, 7, 20

   learning and, 7–9, 20, 32, 40,
         105–107, 113
   retentions and, 6, 34, 35, 113
   student/teacher relationships and,
         6, 8, 32, 36, 39, 40, 58
   students co-learners with, 110
   support and, 24, 139
   supporting personal changes and,
         140–141
Teaching, effective, 37
Technology, 51, 52, 79, 110–112
Testing, x, 6
   African Americans and, 81, 85
   APA and, 34
   cannot take precedence over
         individual learners, 112
   dumbing down instruction and, 35
   economic efficiency and, 133
   home schooling and, 135
   LCPs and, 34–35
   low-income students and, 62
   quality school work and, 74
   scores and, 35, 62, 80, 89, 108 (Figure)
   stress and, 98
   time and, 78
   See also Standards
Thinking:
   context of learning and, 51
   effective LCPs for students in grades
         4–12 and, 89, 90 (Figure)
   higher-order and, 92
   independently, 91–92
   metacognitive factors and, 47.
         See also Metacognitive factors
   motivation and, 52
   strategically, 49–50
   student outcomes and, 108–109
   See also Critical thinking;
         Reflective thinking
Thinking skills, 87, 88 (Figure)
Time factors, 8
   changing, 140
   curriculum and, 63
   effective LCPs for students in K–3
         and, 88
   effects of motivation on effort to learn
         and, 54
   LCPs and, 16
   non-negotiables and, 101
   personal domain and, 19

quality school work and, 74
self-reflections and, 8. *See also*
    Reflective thinking
students/teachers relationships
    and, 40
teachers and, 113
tests and, 78
Tomlinson, C. A., 63, 78
Tomlinson, J., 5
Tompkins, J., 9, 107
Training, 139
Trust, 5
    change and, 137 (Figure)
    classroom management and, 94, 95
    quality school work and, 74
    strategies for creating learner-centered
        classrooms and, 98 (Figure)
    students and, 38
    supporting teachers and, 140–141
Tutoring, 38

Ullman, J., 91
Urban schools:
    achievement gaps and, 81
    caring teachers and, 73, 80, 81, 98, 112
    effective LCPs for students in grades
        4–12 and, 91
    student turnover and, 93
    success and, 64
U.S. Department of Health and Human
    Services, 64, 94

Vakili, D., 32, 52
Valencia, R. R., 85
Valenzuela, A., 85
Values:
    educators and, 71
    LCPs and, 63
    living systems and, 21, 22 (Figure)
    nature of the learning process and, 47
    policies and, 114
Vaughn, A. L., 96
Violence:
    achievement gaps and, 80
    classroom management and,
        94, 95, 96
    ideal high schools and, 98
    mental health and, 96

principle-based approach to, 65
quality school work and, 74
standards and, 17
Vision, 129, 133, 135
Voice, 160
    change and, 107
    classroom management and, 96
    effective LCPs for students in grades
        4–12 and, 91–92
    hearing student and, 148
    non-negotiables and, 104
    support and, 139
    See also Student voices

Wade, P. A., 92
Wagner, T., 97
Wallace, G., 41, 58
Wandersman, A., 65, 94
Watson, M., 36
Watson, T. S., 38
Weinberger, E., 118–119
Weinstein, R. S., 32n 1, 87
Weissberg, R. P., 64, 94
Wheatley, M. J., 17, 18, 19, 114
Whisler, J. S., 31, 32n 1
    anxiety/fear and, 53
    classroom climate and, 75
    developmental/social factors and, 55
    goals and, 48
    learner-centeredness and, 15–16,
        24, 25
    living systems and, 18
    managing change and, 136
    metacognition factors and, 47
    modeling and, 50
    relationships and, 41
Whitaker, K. S., 32n 1
Williams, B., 73, 80
Wilson, B., 73
Wlodkowski, R. J., 157
Wolfe, P., 37
Wolk, R. A., 96
Workshops, 24

Yee, D., 94

Zimmerman, B. J., 4, 47
Zucker, S., 93

CORWIN PRESS

The Corwin Press logo—a raven striding across an open book—represents the union of courage and learning. Corwin Press is committed to improving education for all learners by publishing books and other professional development resources for those serving the field of PreK–12 education. By providing practical, hands-on materials, Corwin Press continues to carry out the promise of its motto: **"Helping Educators Do Their Work Better."**